Ram Ram

Lord Zarathustra

Lord Buddha

Shankaracharya

Sri Ramana Maharishi

Sri Rama Krishna

Annie Besant

I HAVE COME NOT TO TEACH
BUT TO AWAKEN
"MEHER BABA"
AHMED NAGAR.

JOYOUS MYSTICISM IN WORLD RELIGIONS

By

(Late) Yogi Minocher K. Spencer

(Eminent Indian Parsi Yogi, Spiritual seeker, Healer and the author of the rare book of divine experiences of his God realisation: 'HOW I FOUND GOD', 1957)

Abridged & Edited by

Prof. Satya Pal Ruhela

Founder & Secretary

SAI DIVINE CENTRE

126, Sector 37, Faridabad 121 003

Regency Publications

New Delhi

First Published, 1947
Revised Edition, 1998

ISBN 81-86030-72-7

Published by Regency Publications, 20/36-G, Old Market, West Patel Nagar, New Delhi 110 008 and printed at Radiant Printers, New Delhi 110 008, Phones: 574 0038; 571 2539;
• *Telefax: 578 3571.*

DEDICATED

With all reverence and love

to

RISHI RAM RAM

the beloved Master of the Spirit World

who has inspired me to write

this small volume

and

whose loving guidance from the

other world is like a beacon light

in the panorama of Life

Editor's Note

Joyous Mysticism in World Religions is the abridged and edited version of the original book *Joyous Mysticism*, (in two parts) authored by the great Indian Parsi Yogi, Spiritual seeker, Spiritual Healer and God-realised soul Minocher K. Spencer of Karachi (1888-1958). It was first published by the Spiritual Healing Centre, Coimbatore in 1947.

Due to the sudden death of Sri K.S. Aiyer, Secretary and the backbone of the Spiritual Healing Centre in 1965 that Centre abruptly closed down and so this remarkable book on Mysticism has remained out of print and unavailable from the last over thirty years. Since interest in the phenomenon of Mysticism has greatly revived in recent decades in the modern world with mystics like Ramakrishna, Ramana Maharshi, Annie Besant, Sri Shirdi Sai Baba, Sri Meher Baba, Sri Sathya Sai Baba and many others in our country and in the world at large, we have felt that it is hightime that this remarkable classic treatise on Mysticism by the great spiritual seeker Minocher K. Spencer should be republished.

It presents a lucid and comprehensive understanding of the elusive phenomenon of Mysticism and an exhaustive and beautiful survey of the models of Mysticism in all the world religions, from ancient to modern, which can be easily understood by all those who are keenly interested in Mysticism or spiritual mysteries.

As a matter of fact, at some point of time, every one becomes interested in this phenomenon which sheds light on the mysteries of God, supernatural elements, soul and the like, and gives real solace and strength to the man.

We have pleasure in republishing this rare book on mysticism with due editorial treatment, with the kind blessings and encouragement of Sri A. Somasundaram, the 83 year old spiritualist, Founder and Secretary of 'Divine Centre', Markapur (Andhra Pradesh) who was a close friend and confidant of Sri K.S.D. Aiyer, Secretary of the 'Spiritual Healing Centre', Coimbatore and an admirer and friend of Yogi M.K. Spencer. He has, since the closure of the Centre at Coimbatore been inspiringly and dedicatedly carrying forward the unique work of disseminating spiritual knowledge all over the globe under the Presiding Spirit Guides of the 20th Century world— Sri Shirdi Sai Baba, Rishi Ram Ram and Sri Swami Amritanandaji. My grateful thanks are to all these divine personages.

I earnestly hope that this rarest of the rare book on mysticism will be widely read with deep interest by spiritual seekers of all faiths and nationalities and it will immensely benefit them all.

June, 17, 1998

Prof. Satya Pal Ruhela
Professor of Education (Sociology)
Founder & Secretary
SAI DIVINE RESEARCH CENTRE,
126, Sector 37
FARIDABAD 121 003

Contents

INTRODUCTION

As we sit in a secluded corner and behold nature, the thought that arises in our mind is, "There is nothing in this world, but life." The whole universe from the atom to the sky is pulsating with life. And this life is one, though the forms are many. God is one though He manifests Himself in diverse ways. He is the only Reality. The mystic knows this truth by actual experience. There is within him an awareness of God — God who is both transcendental and immanent in nature. It is all radiant light that he sees. His vision takes him to the starry avenue. He climbs the starry ladder step by step till he reaches the abode of the Cosmic Spirit, — God.

Mystics have existed for ages past. They have marched through the corridor of time. Their mysticism has helped this world to go forward in endless ways.

Life is like an endless stream ever flowing from the Unmanifest and going back to the ocean of its origin — God. The mystics understand the secrets of nature. Christ said, "I will utter things which have been kept secret from the foundation of the world." (St. Matthew 13:35). But it is a question whether Christ was really the first to give a new message. What He taught and what demonstrations He gave of His yogic and super-normal powers were no new revelations at all. The yogis and mystics of the ages long before Christ had known the secrets of nature.

Readers will kindly pardon me for making some personal references in regard to the writing of this book. A message was got from Coimbatore, in 1946, that Rishi Ram Ram had selected two of the members of the Spiritual Healing Centre to write books on behalf of the Centre. One of the two selected was myself. I therefore, invoked Rishi Ram Ram on 15th September, 1946, to suggest a title for the book and He gave the following long title: "Joyous Mysticism to lighten mankind into the worship of God" and I was further told: "Write when I inspire you."

This humble work is the result of patient labour. It will be evident that it has not the mark of scholarship, though I was fortunately, in a position to read and study a good number of books, chiefly from the libraries of the local Theosophical Society and the Spiritual Healing Centre, Coimbatore. A fair study of the subject was necessary before Rishi Ram Ram could undertake to inspire me. This book is entirely the result of the Master's inspiration — only the blemishes are mine.

I express my gratitude to my friend in Bombay, who refuses to allow me to disclose his name, for reading the manuscript as usual and for making his observations. I am also grateful to Mr. Phillipowsky, a member of the editorial staff of *The Daily Gazette*, Karachi, for making certain corrections. I am greatly indebted to my dear friend, Mr. Doraswami Iyer, the indefatigable secretary of the Spiritual Healing Centre, Coimbatore, for undertaking to get the book published on behalf of the Centre.

Karachi
24th June, 1947

M.K. Spencer

SECTION I

THE BASICS OF MYSTICISM

1

Mysticism and Religion

What is metaphysics? It is an attempt to conceive and explain the world as a whole, by means of observations and inward feelings. There are people who are rationally minded. To them nothing appeals so much as scientific thought. Newton and Darwin, not to speak of various other scientists, made great scientific discoveries. Their zone of observation was the world, in its outer expression. They subjected everything to rigid classification. They analysed and probed things to their very depths and ultimately derived satisfaction by proclaiming to the world, certain physical laws like gravitation, electricity, material evolution and so forth. But these laws, however applicable they be to forms, fail in their purpose when applied to life. Physical knowledge thus is a limited nature.

Burnett Hillman Street, in his book, "Reality," which is a synthesis of religion and science and a fine critical study of the problems of life says, "As we ascend in the scale of life, any generalisations we can make, any laws we can observe, will necessarily be, not less true, but less complete and exhaustive statements of truth; and the higher we ascend, the more does the relative importance of what they leave unstated to what they succeed in stating continually increase. In the realm of Physics and Chemistry, the generalisations of science fit the facts as exactly as spare parts fit a standard bicycle. When we go to Psychology, though we can still make classifications and discover general laws, they fit the individual case only approximately like a pair of boots ready made. Just as the boot manufacturer tries to secure a better fit by continually producing fresh intermediate sizes, so science is always refining and perfecting its earlier classifications. But to this process there is a necessary limit; at the point where an individual becomes the sole member of his class, the purpose of classification has disappeared." — (Pages 86 and 87)

We reiterate, physical knowledge is incomplete. Its limitation is inherent. Life is not a substance that can be classified or analysed or seen under a microscope. Life can not become an object of knowledge. It is not an entity, that we can compare it to an electron or a molecule. It is a process. It is a ceaseless evolution. Mere scientific knowledge is therefore incomplete. Life is both architect and workman, planner and labourer combined.

What does that mean? Science gives us the knowledge of the mechanism of the universe or things in life. But that which unveils the mystery of nature is man's own intuition or the inward perception. The mystic is the architect, who gives us the design of life's goal and purpose. He unveils to us, God's plan, the nature of the soul, the laws of the spirit, and the relationship of man with the universe and gives us a picture of the journey after death.

Prophets have come to the world and have given their messages from time to time, revealing God's plan and the spiritual heritage of mankind. They have shown the way. Zoroaster, Lord Krishna, Buddha, Moses, Jesus,

Mohamed and others have spoken to men the same truths though in different garbs. Religion is man's best safeguard. It is his greatest consolation in life. It is the pillar, the anchor, the life-buoy in the stormy sea of life's journey. But religion to the ordinary man is based on mere tradition. It is a matter of faith, not experience.

How many are tempted therefore to discard religious truths, owing to the absence of any tangible, provable existence? If there is a God and a life hereafter, what is the proof of it? Mysticism supplies the place. It is religion in practice. God to the mystic is not an entity, that is merely philosophised and talked about by theologians and philosophers. He is a living entity, who can be felt, seen and understood by everyone, only if he or she wishes to do it. Mysticism is the science of the soul, by means of which God can be realised and understood in this very mortal body of flesh and blood.

It is very curious, that though God is infinitely high and measureless, He can become so small as to occupy the small cave of a human heart. It is the heart that is the seat and source of all divinity. It is the seed of divine inspiration. When the heart's strings are strung, a symphony of music is created, the vibrations of which fill the universe. When we are seized with an intense feeling and desire for God, when we think of God and God alone and intensely desire His presence, His guidance and His inspiration, we realize Him. We have only to open the portals of love and the Great Being floods our heart and mind and soul and spirit, with the infinite waves of His holy joy, transforming us into, as if it were, celestial beings. It is through the way of the heart, that we are led to the "unwalled world", the hill of the Lord.

God is Eternal Bliss. The Vedas call Him "*Sat-Chit-Ananda*" (Absolute Existence, Consciousness, Bliss).

"I am the Goal, the Sustainer, the Lord of Witness, the Abode, the Shelter and the Friend, the Origin, Dissolution and Stay, the Treasure house, the Seed Imperishable". (Bhagavad Gita Chapter IX-18)

Just as a man does not become a musician by merely studying the history of the musical instrument but only when he uses it, no one can become an occultist or a mystic by merely reading books on occult literature. God has given to man, a most wondrous instrument — his body — and the human soul, is the musician, the composer, who has to work this instrument and create music out of it. It is the mystic and not the theologian, who through this profound love of God, can unveil the hidden mysteries of Nature and realize God. Spiritual evolution can not be attained by the mere studying of religious books.

God is infinite love. Love is the omnipotence of the Ideal. "To love is to live, to love is to know, to love is to be able, to love is to pray, to love is to be the Man-God." This is what Eliphas Levi in his beautiful book, "The Paradoxes of the Highest Sciences" says: Love is the very essence of religion. It is the pillar and arch of the mystic's heart.

We can not define God. To define Him is to dethrone Him. Faith without understanding is weakness. We only comprehend religion and its vital significance when we practise it, by introspective methods of the mystic. To believe because one knows, is power. To believe without knowledge or understanding, is fruitless and faulty thing.

Jesus said; "And ye shall know the truth and the truth shall make you free". (St. John Chapter 8–32) "Where there is the Spirit of God there is liberty." But we can only achieve truth and liberty by following the mystic's path.

There are potentialities and powers latent in us. We can rise to transcendental heights by the application of our own consciousness or the divinity within us.

The mystic does not rely upon any outside authority. He relies upon his own efforts to reach the transcendental. The burning love for God, the great, deep longing for the Infinite, the intense desire for the Eternal — this is what the mystic feels.

The Dean of St. Paul considers mysticism to be a scientific form of religion.

Religion for the ordinary man as we have said, is based on mere faith. But in the mystic, this faith is transformed into knowledge. Mysticism is based on the testimony of consciousness. Mere teaching of religion by word of mouth can give no assurance of the existence of God or lead to the transcendental knowledge. The mystic's mind is so full of God, that he feels His presence. Ordinarily, there are three kinds of consciousness, which prove the existence of the external world — the bodily, the emotional and the mental consciousness. But in the mystic, there is the fourth consciousness, — the consciousness of the divine within him. He is as if it were *enrapport* with the Divine, which fills his mind, heart and soul with a sublime feeling of joy.

The realm of mysticism is the realm of the Spirit. Religions give us only a part of spiritual knowledge, But the mystic, when he realizes God and thus obtains immortality, finds the door open to the portal of all knowledge. The hidden book of spiritual lore opens out to him. He realizes the unity of life. He gets Cosmic Consciousness.

What is this cosmic consciousness? It is not a mere passing dreaming state, which is awakened in us at some time or the other, by reflection on certain objects, so beautifully described by Tennyson in the following verses:

"Moreover, something is seen or seems,
That touches one with mystic gleams
Like glimpses of forgotten dreams—
Of something felt, like something here
Of something done, I know not where;
Such as no language may declare."

Sometimes, even by mechanical means the state of joyous self-forgetfulness is obtained, such as when man is intoxicated with wine or he is given some drug like nitrous oxide and ether sufficiently diluted with air. But such experiences should not be mistaken for the mystic's true state of inward joyousness. They are degraded type of consciousness.

There are some records of mystical experiences with chloroform. The following statement of experience by a patient would be of some interest:

"All the choking and stifling had passed away. I seemed at first in a state of utter blankness; then came flashes of intense light, alternating with blankness and with a keen vision of what was going on in the room around me, but no sensation of touch. I thought I was near death, when suddenly my soul became aware of God, who was manifestly dealing with me, so to speak, in the intense personal present reality. I felt Him streaming in like light upon me — I can not describe the ecstasy I felt. Then as I gradually awoke from the influence of the anaesthetic, the old sense of my relation to the world began to return, the new sense of my relation to God began to fade. I suddenly leapt to my feet on the chair where I was sitting and shrieked out, "It is too horrible, it is too horrible, it is too horrible" — meaning that I could not bear this disillusion. Then I flung myself on the ground and at last awoke covered with blood, calling to the two surgeons (who were frightened). "Why did you not kill me? Why did you not let me die?" Only think of it. To have felt for that long dateless ecstasy of vision the very God in all purity and tenderness and truth and absolute love and then to find that I had after all no revelation but that I had been tricked by the abnormal excitement of the brain". (*The Varieties of Religious Experiences* by William James — page 391)

The above experience of the patient should not be considered as the result of any "abnormal excitement of the brain". In fact, the patient himself corrects this mistake, by further proceeding to say: "Yes, this question remains — Is it possible that the inner sense of reality which succeeded, when my flesh was dead to impressions from without to the ordinary sense of physical relations, was not a delusion but an actual experience? Is it possible that in that moment I felt what some of the saints have said they always felt, the undemonstrable but irrefragable certainty of God". (William James. *The Varieties of Religious Experiences*, page 392)

What we feel is, that in the anaesthetic stage, as in sleep, the soul leaves the body and makes an excursion into the "Other Worlds". Generally the impressions of such excursions are forgotten when the soul returns to the body, in its waking state. But in some extraordinary cases the impressions are not forgotten and the above case quoted is of that latter category. The patient was able to remember his excursion into the astral world and was naturally sorry to have come back to this physical, mundane plane.

But such types of anaesthic revelations should not be mixed up with cosmic consciousness which is of the superb type and which leaves a permanent impression on the mind and creates a feeling of mystical joy of a transcendental order.

Cosmic consciousness is not merely an expansion or extension of the conscious mind. It is consciousness of the cosmos, of the life of the universe. It elevates the soul and places it on an exalted level. It fills the mind with an inexpressible feeling of delight. It enhances intellectual powers. It brings a sense of immortality — a consciousness of eternal life. It gives a feeling of unity of life — the oneness of God with His entire creation.

God is absolute transcendency and mysticism is an endeavour of the human mind to grasp the ultimate Reality, to probe the essence and secrets of the cosmos and to enjoy transcendental bliss even when in physical life.

Let us explain at length the distinctive marks of mysticism.

The first is its effability. The mystic state is one, which defies definition. It is a state of consciousness which can not be transferred, reported or explained. It has to be felt, just like a lover knows what love is, when he is in love with his beloved. It is a direct experience, the contents of which can not be imparted or explained to any one. Intellect seems to swoon away in the highest states of ecstasy. The man loses all consciousness of time, space and causality. Everything seems to be absorbed in one Reality that is God, which is all Light — transcendental Light of the Highest radiance and all joy. The mystic's attitude is that of self-surrender. The world appears to him as a fleeting fantasy. All is unreal except God, who is the only Reality.

The second distinctive mark of mysticism is its noetic quality. Mysticism is not only a state of emotion, it is also a state of mind. Love and Thought — these are the keys of the mystic's realm. William James, a famous lecturer on Religion and the author of *The Varieties of Religious Experiences* says, "Although so similar to states of feeling, mystical states seem to those who experience them to be also states of knowledge. They are states of insight into depths of truth unplumbed by the discursive intellect. They are illuminations, revelations, full of significance and importance, all inarticulate though they remain; and as a rule they carry with them a curious sense of authority for after-time." (pages 380 and 381)

The third characteristic is that the state of ecstatic bliss does not last long. Half an hour, an hour or, at most, two hours is generally the limit, though we know of certain Indian yogis, who can go into '*samadhi*' for hours, days and months together. The Hindus call this extreme state of meditation, *samadhi*. This exquisite state occurs over and over again, bringing inner gladness.

The fourth significant trait of the mystic mind is its submissiveness — the state of passivity. The mystic feels, that he is held as if it were by a superior power. Mysticism develops all the feminine traits in a man's character — as opposed to masculine, he becomes submissive, humble, gentle, patient, reticent, silent, meek and kind. He is seldom obtrusive or self-assertive. He prefers to keep in the back-ground. He seldom argues or discusses. His silence is ethereal. His humility is sublime.

There is a considerable resemblance between mysticism and music. Both are divine, both defy definition, both allude to harmony and peace In the words of Clifford Harrison, "Mysticism is in the world of thought, what music is in the world of sound." — (*Notes on the Margin*)

The mystic knows that God is both immanent and transcendent. He is the Absolute, all pervading, indwelling Spirit. To a pantheist, God is only immanent. But the mystic, though he understands, that God dwells within the innermost recesses of his heart, thinks, that he is separate also and his aim is to seek union with that Supreme Being who, is, as it were alien, from him. His heart's desire is union with the Supreme Being.

Mysticism is an inward state, inborn and innate in man. As Jalal-uddin Rumi says, "The astrolabe of the mysteries of God is love." It is the mystic's love and devotion to God, which plays the important part in the acquirement of divine knowledge. The astronomer for his astronomical discoveries wants the equipment of spectroscope and a sixty inch reflector. But the mystic's instrument is the inward eye, the burning love for God. Is it not said in the Bible,"Blessed are the pure in heart for they shall see God?" (St. Matthew. 5–8)

Just as a disease can not be cured by pronouncing the name of medicine, but by actually taking it, any number of parrot-like repetitions of the name of God, can not bring us to the realisation of God. It is only the true mystic, that can realize him. Metaphysics is a science, good for study. Mysticism is a direct experience of God. As Sankara says, "The nature of the Reality must be known by one's own clear spiritual perception; it can not be known through a *pandit* (a learned man). Similarly the form of the moon can only be known through one's own eyes. How can it be known through others?"

"When a man follows the way of the world, or the way of the flesh or the way of tradition, i.e. when he believes in religious rites and the letters of the scriptures, as though they were intrinsically sacred, knowledge of the Reality can not arise in him." (Sankara)

The scriptures speak of the outward man and the inner man. The outward man is the old man, who depends upon his senses. He is the earthly man. But the inner man, is the new man, the heavenly man, the young man, who rises above the senses. "I live yet not I, but the Christ — the eternal Logos — liveth in me". It is when we purge ourselves of all the gross in us, that we are made channel by the higher ones, to receive the grace of God within us.

The mystic considers the world as a delusion. God being the only Reality, he craves union with Him. He is not satisfied by mere historical revelations or religious teachings. He is animated by his own impulses and emotions. He is derided by the ignorant. His feats of trances and snatches of exquisite bliss are ridiculed and condemned as brutish torpor or excitement of the nerves. Such outbursts of ignorance are most nauseating. Such ignorant critics deserve to be pitied, for they know not what harm they do to their own spirit.

There is still a large section of human population, who look upon mystics as cranks or crooks. Meher Baba is a mystic, more maligned than any one, that we know of. He is an Iranian of short stature, fair, with beaming eyes and black flowing hair, of robust constitution — a beautiful and pleasant personality. Contact with him creates confidence. He radiates joy. If there be any doubt, it is soon dispelled by the mystic's glance. His child like simplicity, his utter frankness, his look of love, his joyous smile, his naturalness in every manoeuvre or action, his humility, his docility, make a strong impression. One cannot agree with the picture that Paul Brunton draws of this mystic sage of Ahmednagar, (India) in his book, — *The Secret Path*. The very fact that he has been able to observe the silence of a sphinx for the last so many years, is a great achievement in itself.

Silence is a matter of inward conviction. To ridicule Meher Baba and say that he is observing silence, because he has no new knowledge to give and that his silence is a sheet, by which he covers his own ignorance, is a great sin.

We shall not discuss the question, whether Meher Baba can be accepted as the world's next prophet. When he was asked by me what his mission was, he said, "To make people know and experience that they are all one in the divine." Every one is a prophet in the making. This reminds us of what Christ himself said to his followers, "I and my Father are one, and ye also, who are His children, shall be one with Him."

We shall not enter into any discussion about Meher Baba's teachings or his competence to claim his spirituality, as a prophet. The following spirit message received at the altar of the Spiritual Healing Centre, at Coimbatore, which is the Mecca of spiritualists, India, is of considerable import:

"He (Meher Baba) is a highly evolved spiritual person with rare insight and wisdom. The inspiration of meeting a person of spiritual greatness often thrills and exalts. In some, the contact opens the inner vision. The disciple should have evolved high to benefit by such contacts. The ripe fruit falls off from worldliness and low life by the mere touch of a saint, but not the unripe in spiritual development."

Another living saint and mystic in India, of a far greater renown is Bhagwan Sri Ramana of Arunchala. When he was a lad, studying in school, he did not show himself to be diligent in his studies. There was nothing very remarkable about him, except that, there was a thirst in him for spiritual knowledge.

One day, all of a sudden, he was seized with a desire to renounce life, to leave his home and live in the temple of Arunachala, a place that was at a distance from his city.

How this great awareness of God came to him at such a young age, when boys are generally full of mischief and pranks is a mystery. Not initiated by any guru, without any special training or knowledge, without having come into contact with any saint or sage, he had this inward feeling to leave his home, in "search of his Father." He bought a third class ticket to go to the temple of Arunachala. When he arrived after having tramped a long distance on foot, from the last railway station, he was physically exhausted. But we can understand the depth of his feelings and the serenity of his mind, from the following words, which he gave utterance to, as soon as he was received in the temple:

"O Lord, obedient to Thy call
Have I come deserting all,
No boon I ask, no loss bemoan,
Take me in and make Thine own"

He arrived at the temple on first September, 1896, and, from that date to this date, he has never moved out to any place. The jubilee of his fifty years' stay in Arunachala was celebrated in 1946. It is a unique record of transcendental life. Of all the tributes paid to this God-realized man, a few extracts from the illuminating article contributed by Sadhu Ekarasa, (Dr. G.H. Mees, M.A., Ph.D.) to the golden jubilee volume would not be out of place:

"If a man were to do the greatest deed in the world and come and sit in the presence of Bhagwan Sri Ramana Maharshi, he would realize that his deed was as nothing compared to the perpetual deed of self-realization of the sage."

"If a man were to write the greatest book in the world and come and lay it as an offering before the sage, he would realize, that the sage was a greater book, which was written from day to day, not with the medium of pen and ink and paper, but without intermediation and even without any conscious effort, in the inner being of all who care to come and read it.

"The Maharshi is above the spirit of the time. Long after the spirit of the time will have been succeeded by the spirit of another age, Sri Ramana Maharshi will be remembered as an immortal. His immortality stands out from his every word and look. It lives in the inner heart of all who have had the great privilege to come and sit in his presence.

"Sri Ramana proclaims that life is full of latent happiness for those whose lot it is to struggle with the most distressing propensities to the *Samsara*, because the Divine Heritage is ever there, waiting to be received. God-reality is ever present within the heart of all. The act of full surrender of the man of darkness to the Lord of Light is bound to reveal it, as the dawn dispels the darkness of the night. And just as the dawn is not the first dawn, but reveals the eternal light of the sun, the dawn of Self-realisation is not a new creation, but the remembering of a last state of consciousness. It is an entering into the ancient heritage."

Sri Ramana's teaching is not a new one. It is as ancient as the hills. It is the common note of all mystics, that we have descended from God and we all shall ascend again to God.

When Maharshi was asked, why he preferred to remain at one place and avoided speaking from public platforms, maintaining silence all the time, he replied: "Silence is eternal speech, that state which transcends speech and thought is *Mouna* (Silence); it is meditation without mental activity. Subjugation of the mind is meditation; deep meditation is eternal speech. Silence is ever speaking; it is perennial flow of language. It is interrupted by speaking; for words obstruct this mute language."

As Browning says in his *Paracelsus*;

"That is inmost centre in us all
Where truth abides in fullness; and around
Wall upon wall, the gross flesh hems it in
This perfect clear conception — which is truth."

It is the flesh that hides the truth. It is our desire and passions that seek mastery over ourselves and separate us from the Reality.

This Reality is something that is super-splendent, super-essential, super-sublime. It is super-everything that can be named, as William James puts it. The mystic wants to reach this positive pole of truth by the method of negation, which is so commonly resorted to by Vedantists. The Absolute is so beyond our comprehension, that every application of an adjective is denied. As soon as an attempt is made to describe the Absolute in any the most hyperbolic language, we dethrone the Self.

The Christian mystic, Dionysius the Areopagite describes the Absolute by means of negation thus:

"The cause of all things is neither soul nor intellect; nor has it imagination, opinion or reason or intelligence;

nor is it reason or intelligence, nor is it spoken or thought. It is neither number, nor order, nor magnitude, nor littleness, nor equality, nor inequality, nor similarity, nor dissimilarity. It neither stands, nor moves, nor rests. It is neither essence, nor eternity, nor time. Even intellectual contact does not belong to it. It is neither science nor truth."

The prime Love is compared to Nothing for it is not comprehensible by anything:

So infinite is the Godhead, that even the highest imagination can not portray it in any language. The mystic therefore when he passes from the ordinary consciousness into the higher consciousness, feels his ascent from the lower world into a higher world, from smallness into vastness. The predominant note of all mystical experiences is that of healthy, vital optimism. To worship God, who is the Highest and Super-excellent, is to feel a joyousness beyond compare. Mysticism is joyousness which lightens mankind to the worship of God. Just as water poured out into water, becomes water, fire becomes fire, and earth becomes earth, when man longs intensely for God — the subject and object become one — he becomes united with God.

This is the teaching of all the different schools of mystics in different climes and different ages. The very fact of the identity of mystic teachings in various countries of the world, gives to mysticism a stamp of veracity of no common nature.

Pythagoras said, "All come from one, God embraces all and actuates all, yet is but one." The same thought is expressed in different garb by Bruno, the great scientist and mystic, who as we know was burnt to death by religious fanatics. "Understand then", he said, "that all things, are in the universe and the universe in all things, us in that and that in us and so all meet in one perfect unity." Spinoza says, also, nearly to the same effect; "The absolute self-existent substance is God; everything else must be attributes and modes under which that substance appears. There can be no real existence outside. He is the universal All." Emerson, the great American mystical thinker, also gives expression to the same thought, when he says: "The day of days, the great day of the feast of life is that in which the inward eye opens to the unity of things."

Schopenhaner, the great German philosopher, pays an eloquent tribute to the mystics in the following words:

"Nothing is more astonishing than the unanimity of all who profess these principles, notwithstanding the greatest diversity of age, country and religion. They do not form a sect; indeed, they are mostly ignorant of each others' existence. The Indian, Christian and Mohammedan mystics, quietists and ascetics are desperate in all things, only not in their inner spirit and meaning of their teachings. So much concord, among such divergent peoples and time, is practical proof that theirs' is not a distorted and perverted state of mind but an expression of essential constituent of human nature, whose rarity is solely due to its excellence."

There is absolutely nothing in "mysticism" of a shadowy nature. To identify "mysticism" and "occultism", as subjects that deal in ghosts and such midnight spectral appearances is most misleading and erroneous. In fact, as we have already explained mysticism is a transcendental subject. One writer calls it, —"physical experience transcendentalised." It must also be remembered, that mystics, though they appear to be dreamy, are the most practically-minded people. Clifford Harrison says in his book, *Notes on the Margin*, "The mystics are terribly practical people, quiet students and devotees as they may seem. They go or seem to go own to the roots of things after a way of their own and lay foundation on which those who come after them can not choose but build as we are building now."

Jamshed Nusserwanji, "the Builder of Modern Karachi" is a mystic and yet it would be hard to beat him, in his practicality.

When we cast a glance at the history of religion, we shudder to think of the many scientists and people of honest conviction that were dragged out and burnt by religious fanatics. Mysticism has no such horrid record. It has not burnt a Bruno; it has not forced a Gallileo to recant his honest convictions. It has enshrined and consecrated all that is best in religion. It has given its welcome and acceptance to the discoveries of science and history. Claude Bernard says, "I am persuaded that a day will come in which the physiologist, the poet and the philosopher will speak the same language and will understand one another."

Mysticism is a blend of poetry, philosophy and all that is best in human nature. Evolution is not a mere growth or a process. It is, as Dr. Annie Besant says, the unfolding of the powers latent in man. Mysticism holds a key to the inner researches of the human heart, which is the abode of God. It speaks in universal language. Its breath is God; its gospel is unity of life.

We all have in us a hidden life, a latent consciousness, a second sight, a sort of a superior soul. The existence of this superior soul is often unknown to us and to our friends. It lives, it suffers, it fights and when it succeeds in liberating itself, it is by its own innate efforts, without cognisance of external life. The whole process is inward. It is an inward fight against the crushing weight of hard, stony external, phenomenal life.

Faith, Love and Hope, form the triad of the mystic's philosophy. It is on this foundation that the whole superstructure is raised. Faith in God, the Absolute, is the key to the mystical life. It is the faith, which helps him to rise above all dogmas and creeds. It is this faith which explains all phenomena.

Love is the most vital principle in spirituality. It plays an important role in physical life, but in the inward, higher life, it is a *sine-qua-non.* It is the most potent instrument. God is infinite love. "To love is to live, to love is to know, to love is to be able, to love is to be the man-God." And it is through faith and love of God and all mankind, that the mystic hopes and dreams of the final achievement, namely, union with the Divine Being.

Mysticism covers a long range of subjects. It includes Occultism, Spiritualism, Psychism, Alchemy, Necromancy, Freemasonry, Mesmerism, and so forth. We have a plethora of literature on the subject. The various schools and cults have made contributions, — the Magi of Iran, the Yogis of India, the Hierophants of Egypt, the Sufis of Islam, the Essenes of Judaea, the Pythagoreans and the Platonists of Greece, the Neo Platonists of Alexandria, the Kabalists, the Theosophists, the Rosicrucians and the Gnostics, the Pietists and Quietists of the church, the Templars of the Middle ages, the French Encyclopaedistes — the German Mystics, the Swedenborgians, the early Quakers and the Cambridge Platonists. To write a history of Mysticism would be useless, not because it is exhaustive, but it would not be justified, as "every man is his own mystic." We shall in the succeeding chapters just glance at the teachings and methods of some of the important schools, more with a view to prove the identity of their conclusions and achievements, than anything else.

2

Matter and Spirit

It is the firm conviction of the mystic that All is one and one is All. The origin of the whole creation is God, who is the Absolute Spirit. He breathed out a word and the universe was formed. The Invisible became visible. "Things which are seen are made out of things which are unseen", says the Bible. In the *Rig Veda-Samhita* which is considered to be the oldest book of the world, it is said, "Not-being and Being are in the highest heaven in the birth-place of Daksha, in the lap of *Aditi.*"

"In the first age of the gods, Being (Comprehensible Deity) was born from non-Being (whom no intelligence can comprehend) after it were born the Regions (the invisible) from them *uttanapada.*

"From *Uttanapada* the Earth was born. The Regions (those that are visible) were born from the Earth. *Daksha* was born of *Aditi* and *Aditi* from *Daksha.*"

The ancients were quite convinced, from what we can understand from the scriptures, that spirit and its manifestations, energy and force pervaded the whole universe and that God, the Invisible, from whom emanated all the forces and all the substances, by whatever name they be called, in their external manifestations is the Absolute Spirit, boundless, measureless, eternal, without beginning, without end. The spiritual knowledge of the Ancients was put to a hard test, when man began to evolve mentally and scientists came out with their discoveries one by one. The first shock to religion was Newton's discovery of the physical laws, especially of gravitation. Later on, Darwin brought out his book — "*Origin of Species*" and the theory of evolution on the physical plane made a tremendous stir. Rationalism and intellectualism had sway and religion got a terrific set-back.

When Laplace wrote a treatise on astronomy, he was asked why God was nowhere mentioned. And his reply was a classical expression of the thought of the peoples of that time. He said: "Sire, I have no need of that hypothesis." Darwin taught that consciousness was only an "epiphenomenon", a functionless shadow cast by automatic changes in that material process which is the sole reality."

Even when spiritualism made its advent in Europe, a few decades ago, after it had made a stir in America, where it was first born, our hard-hearted scientists made a fierce attack on the movement. But the recent discoveries of science, completely refute the theories which were once claimed by the scientists, as true. The atom, supposed to be the ultimate unit of matter and to be a solid substance, is recognised now by Physics, as some sort of force or energy. It is made of electrons and protons. The electrons revolve round a centre known as a proton. Matter in the last stage is electric force.

The Theory of Relativity propounded by Einstein has given a further shattering blow to the materialistic concept of universe. Bertrand Russell says, "The theory of relativity by merging time into space has damaged the traditional notion of substance more than all the arguments of the philosophers. Matter for commonsense, is something which persists in time and moves in space. The old solidity is gone."

Science has now proved to the hilt that matter and spirit give one form, thanks to the discovery of the atomic bomb in the last European war. It would not be incorrect to say that both spirit and matter are the two ends of the same thing, one end is visible, the other is invisible, just like ice and vapour. Matter in fact is the densest part of spirit. There is no separation between spirit and matter.

God is one and His Spirit pervades throughout the universe. Look at the extraordinary intricate machinery of His Plan. According to Dr. Millikan, "one million atoms can be placed on the diameter of a head of a pin. Inside of each atom is a nucleus one ten-thousandth the diameter of an atom. Arranged about the necleus, in the case of the metal, uranium, are 92 electrons, and inside of this nucleus are exactly 238 positions and 146 negratrons. If one electron is added or removed, it becomes some other metal. Matter is thus formed of electrons and electrons are formed of cosmic substance spirit, energy of life."

Take another example. The earth is composed of 92 chemicals and all these chemicals are formed of one original, primordial, cosmic element — the electrons. Is it not very pithily said. "Electrons are the building blocks of the universe?"

All nature is a living thought. The angels speak in the language of thought. The mystic communes with the invisible by means of inward consciousness. His realm is the realm of the Spirit. He knows what is real and what is not real. He knows the limitations of the senses.

In the *Bhagvad Gita,* a whole chapter is devoted (Discourse XVI) to Spirituality and Materialism. "There are two creations of being in this world, the divine and the demoniac (Discourse XVI–6).

"Fearlessness, Purity of heart, steadfastness in knowledge, Yoga, alms-giving, self-restraint, study of one's own scriptures, austerity, uprightness, harmlessness, truth, absence of anger, renunciation, serenity, absence of calumny, compassion to creatures, uncovetousness, gentleness, modesty, absence of fickleness, energy, forgiveness, fortitude, purity, absence of hatred, absence of pride — these belong", says the Gita,"to one born for divine lot." They give liberation. (XVI–3).

The demoniac qualities which give bondage arc according to the Gita, "Ostentation, arrogance, self-conceit, insolence, ignorance, insatiable desires, hypocrisy, sensual enjoyment, lust, love for wealth, energy, egotism, haughtiness, anger, malice and greed." They lead to the regions of darkness. (XVI–4).

Man is his eager desire to gain happiness runs after the pleasures of the senses, little knowing that they are of fleeting nature. The most important is often overlooked. Is it not said in the Bible, "Enter ye in at the strait gate: for wide *is* the gate and broad *is* the way, that leadeth to destruction, and many there be which go in there at:

Because strait *is* the gate, and narrow *is* the way, which leadeth unto life, and few there be that find it". (St. Mathew–VII–13 and 14)

We are all so dominated by the senses, that we allow them to get a hold on us. But if desires which are the root causes of the bondage, are annihilated we get nearer to the mystic's goal of inward joyousness, which is a quality of the soul and not of the body.

The Gita speaks of three *gunas* — *Satva, Rajas* and *Tamas. Satva* is harmony. It is a spiritual quality. It is the highest in man. It brings peace and joyousness which are divine — the fruit of *Nishkama. Rajas* is action. The *Rajasic* people are those who work for ostentation, for reward and return. *Tamas* is the lowest quality in man. It is sloth, indolence, lust — the depravity of the soul.

According to Bhagvad Gita, God is so merciful, that if He chooses, He can allow even repentant sinners a chance to be liberated from the bondage of life.

"Should even a great sinner revere Me only and Love Me above all, he is to be considered a good one, as he will attain the truth. Such a one will soon set out on the right path and shall attain the eternal peace. Be convinced, that he who reveres Me, in truth, shall not perish, for he who takes refuge in Me, O Partha, treads the highest path, be he a woman, a husbandman or a servant and should he have started in sins." (Bhagvad Gita IX–29 to 31)

We may give a few historical instances of men, who started their lives as pleasure seekers and became saints, philosophers and sages. The most illustrious example is that of Asoka. He was a libertine in his young age. But he soon got weary of sensuous pleasures. In the history of India, we do not know of a better ruler than Asoka and among the followers of the great Buddha, we do not know of any one who did more to propagate his teachings than Asoka. After he had quelled all the disturbing elements in the country and welded the disintegrant parts, into a homogeneous whole, giving the distracted people a sense of safety, security, peace and prosperity, the warrior sheathed his sword and took to a life of rigid austerity, practising the teachings of Lord Buddha to the very letter and spirit. We are told that eventually he was so overcome with the thought of self-annihilation that he went away to a jungle, advising his men, not to follow him, but to allow him to disappear in complete darkness to gain his nirvanic bliss. Upto the moment, no historian has been able to give the date of his death or the place at which he died. He came from the void; he returned to the void.

Who does not know of St. Augustine? In his young age, the drinking bouts and other sensuous pleasures filled the programme of his day. But these pleasures became so distasteful to him, that his soul at last revolted. He saw the folly of the poison, he was swallowing day by day, and bitterly repented for the sins committed in ignorance of the great Reality, viz. God. He turned over a new leaf and became a saint.

Count Leo Tolstoy in his young age was a pleasure-loving fellow. But the suffering of the poor that he saw around him soon awakened his dormant conscience. He could not reconcile himself to the thought that he should be so rich and be fed with all the luxuries of life while his poor tenants on the farms and the fields should go hungry and naked. He felt the impulse of his heart. He took to a life of austerity and poverty. He cobbled his own shoes. He tilled the land himself. Being a great literary genius, he wrote revolutionary books. He was never frightened of the Government, which he knew was tyrannical and, therefore, exposed its policy of economical exploitation of the dumb masses. He would have given away all his wealth to the poor, but for the obstinacy of his wife, who opposed him, in the interest of her children. Tolstoly's love for the poor was so great, that he died peacefully in the cottage of a humble peasant labourer outside his princely palace. To serve the poor is to be cognizant of the voice of God within, to feel His joy, His divinity.

We may take one more example. Plato was a rich man's son and he inherited a large estate. He took to a life of pleasure. He was fond of beauty and had a gift for writing verses. He had a large circle of friends and admirers who praised his poetical talents and enjoyed his sumptuous banquets.

One day, this great Athenian passing by, heard Socrates preaching to the youths of Athens in the street. "Goodness is better than beauty and truth is better than goodness. For you can perceive truth and goodness in the depth of the human soul and nowhere else."

Plato was struck. The words awakened a new thought in his mind. They inflamed his heart. He resolved there and then to change his attitude of mind and to pursue the path of truth and goodness. He called his friends to a big banquet. When the banquet was over, he collected his guests in the big hall studded with pictures of art and statues of exquisite design. Plato was a poet; he brought the manuscripts of all the beautiful poems that he had written and said to his friends, "This is the last of my banquets. I say from today, good-bye to all the pleasures of the senses. That man in the street who goes by the name of Socrates has captivated my heart. He has taught me, that goodness is greater than beauty and truth is greater than goodness. Truth and goodness are the marks of the human soul. I am going to make a bonfire of these manuscripts for no more shall I write poems but I shall become a devout student of God, leading a life of austerity. Philosophy shall be my bride — not poetry." With these words, he applied a burning match to the heaps of paper, to the utter dismay of his friends, who admired his poems. Plato, the poet was extinct from that day; we know him now as one of the finest philosophers and mystic writers of the world.

We have shown in this chapter that matter has no permanent place in the universe. It is only an outward, fleeting expression of that which is eternal and which is invisible. It is the densest part of the spirit which alone has cosmic value. Just as everything in nature resolves into spirit-energy-force, man has also to discard the realm of the senses and gather his strength by purity of mind and inward cogitation to achieve unity with God, which is the goal of life. It is by knowing ourselves, that we can get rid of the outer crust of matter and enter into the path of the spirit, which must lead us on to the various stages of initiation, ending in the goal of the soul's absorption into the Highest Spirit. Is it not said, "O man, know thyself, in the is hid the treasurer of treasures."

When Buddha died he gave expression to the following most significant statement:

"All compounds are perishable. Spirit is the sole, elementary and primordial unity and each of its rays is immortal, infinite and indestructible. Beware of the illusions of matter."

Buddha warns us of the illusion of matter. The same thought is expressed in a very beautiful manner, with plenty of poetical imagery by Madame Blavatsky in her immortal work — *The Voice of the Silence.* She says,"If thy soul smiles, while bathing in the sunlight of thy life; if thy soul sings within her chrysalis of flesh and matter; if thy soul weeps inside her castle of illusion; if thy soul struggles to break the silver thread that binds her to the Master, know, O, disciple, thy soul is of the earth."

We have to look at the matter with the eyes of the spirit. Matter is mere shadow, spirit is substance. Matter is earthy; Spirit is divine. Matter is the external world; Spirit is the internal realm. The external and internal experiences are necessary for attainment of our goal.

Matter and Spirit are the two opposites. Matter is passive, feminine, it does not move of its own self. It has no light of its own. It is a negative force. Spirit is a masculine principle. It is active, it is all-pervading, it is creative, it is energetic.

Man is made of the higher self and the lower self — the higher *manas* and the lower *manas*. The higher triad is composed of *atma*, *buddhi* and *manas*. It is the spiritual ego. The lower self is composed of body, emotions and the lower *manas*, that is lower mind. So long as the soul dwells and keeps itself attached to the lower clothing, as Madame Blavatsky says, it may attain temporary happiness — "The soul smiles while bathing in the sunlight of thy life." But the soul is tied with a silver thread with the higher triad namely, *atma*, *buddhi* and *manas* (higher mind) and this should not be snapped. If the silver thread that binds the soul to the Master, (the guide, of whom we shall speak later on in a separate chapter) is snapped it will become earthy and will not hear the voice of the inner self, which is God within.

Experiences of external life are necessary and therefore external phenomena play an important role in the adventure of life's pilgrimage, the goal of which is God-realization. But we repeat, that we must understand that matter after all is a delusion and an illusion and we must endeavour to look at every thing with the internal perception, with the eyes of the spirit.

The *Gita* speaks of harmonising matter with spirit, *Prakritti* with *Purusha*, the external world with the internal world, keeping in mind, the fact that God can be realised by getting experiences of the external by the use of spiritual eyes. Non-attachment to the world is the key to the solution of the life's problem.

The five senses — hearing, touch, sight, taste and smell to which may be added the lower mind, which is the sixth sense —these are to be transcended, to be slain, if Reality, which is the goal, is to be achieved. The destruction of the sense of individuality is the first step in the path of Initiation. The senses are the slayers of the Real. Says Madame Blavatsky:

> "The Mind is the great Slayer of the Real
> Let the disciple slay the slayer."
>
> (*Voice of the silence.*)

Just as there are physical laws, there are spiritual laws. Man is inter-woven with the sense world and the inner world. He is the product of nature and its laws, but he has also within him, this spark of God — which is immortal and which is above the laws.

Matter is finite. It is by transcending the finite that God, who is Infinite can be realized.

Arthur Edward Waite, the author of *The Occult Science* says: "The mode of transcending the phenomenal world, as taught by the mystics, consists, and to some extent exclusively, of a form of intellectual ascension or development, which is equivalent to a concise application of selective evolutionary laws by man himself to man."

The object and ideal of the alchemists of the middle ages was to achieve by direct means God-consciousness, by exalting and transmuting the lower self into higher self. Incidentally, the alchemists laid the foundation of the science of Chemistry, but it must be said, that they were originally concerned with the question of the growth of the soul and to avoid harassment and persecution by the wily priestcraft of the Christian Church, they were compelled to use symbological language to hide their higher pursuit. The philosopher's stone which was the object of search by the alchemists was not, as was thought by the common people, any instrument for transmuting the lower metal into gold. The alchemists were spiritual philosophers and their search was for God, by direct experience. The Philosopher's stone is a symbolic or allegorical expression for God-realization. The other symbols profusely used by the alchemists were sulphur, by which they meant human conscience, mercury, which represented the spirit of God in man while lead and antimony were used to indicate man's unregenerated nature.

There are three natures in man. There is, first, the animal-man in man. When he leads the life of the senses and does not care for any higher values, he is of the lower animal type. The other man is the inner man, when man begins to think and realize the importance of rational living. The third, and the highest in man, is the spiritual man, when he hungers for spiritual food and thought. When a man can feel that the eye with which he sees God, is the eye with which God sees him, that his eye and God's eye are the same, he reaches that perfection, which is the alchemy of life.

Is it not said in the Bible, "It is the spirit that quickeneth; the flesh profiteth nothing" (St. John. Chapter VI–63).

"Form, personality and sensuality are the death of spirit; the dissolution of form, loss of personality and unconsciousness of sensuous perceptions render spirit free and restore it to life" (*Magic, White and Black* by Dr. Franz Hartman, page 250).

Buddha says, "The permanent never mingles with the impermanent although the two are one. Only when all outward appearances are gone, is left that one principle of life which exists independently of all external phenomena. It is the fire that burns within the external light when the fuel is expended and the flame is extinguished, for that fire is neither in the flame nor in the fuel, not yet inside either of the two, but above, beneath and everywhere."

As is observed in the Bible "In the beginning was the word, the word was God and the word was with God" signifying God in spirit and His manifestation in matter.

When we observe nature with the eyes of intellect, we say that there is a duality. Everything that we call "Life," or "Energy" is a duality. But this duality is ephemeral for All is One. This One in a state of vibration produced a multiple of forms but these forms are journeying to and fro and their ultimate destiny is to re-unite with the original One Life. Desires originate from a sense of duality bringing suffering and it is only, when we leave the path of condensation and fly to the original unity, that peace and tranquillity reign triumphant. Matter is an illusion; it is by the way of the spirit within us, when real awakening comes, shall we march on to the realisation of the Absolute. We have to carry this consciousness throughout all the planes of our being.

It is the heart that understands the divine language. It is there the vibrations of the One are heard; it is there the vision of the One is seen.

The mystics speak in the language of symbols. The following symbol of double triangles so commonly used by hieorophants and mystics of all ages and countries and in modern times by the Theosophists illustrate the teaching of the law of involution and evolution — the descent of the spirit from the Original Source into matter and the ascent of matter to Spirit.

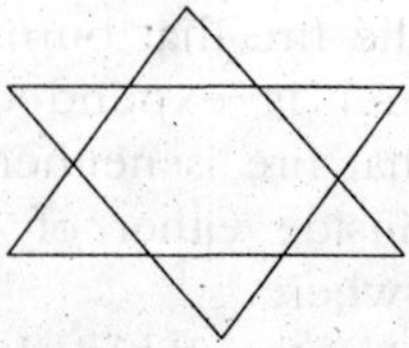

There is another symbol most commonly used and that is the Cross. It should not be understood that the symbol of the Cross came in vogue from the time of Jesus Christ, who was crucified on the Cross. It was known long, long ago. It was found in the ancient cave temples of Egypt and India. The four ends of the Cross are the four elements viz. Earth, Water, Fire and Air. The Horizontal line represents the animal principle, for all animals bow down to the earth. But man alone stands erect and it is, therefore that he is represented by the perpendicular line — the line of divinity. When man transgresses the laws of nature, he must suffer and the Cross represents his suffering. But eventually he must go back to God and the Cross symbolises, his crucial trial on earth, as well as realization of Truth, which is God.

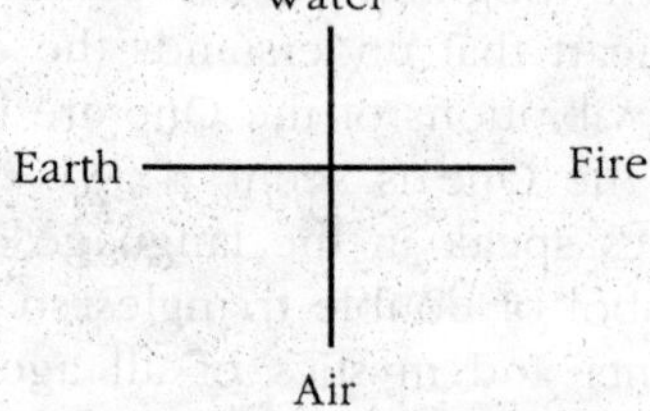

To know, to will, to dare and to be silent, these are the four-fold ways of dissolving matter and absorbing one-self in the Spirit. We shall refer to the various stages and methods of this process in the subsequent chapters.

3

The Reality: Occultism

The quest of man is God. There is not a man who at some time or the other in life could not have felt an urge to solve the mystery of life by rending the veil that hides the secrets of the universe. It is true that the majority of us lead life, as it cometh, without much bothering to know what it portends to be, what is the goal of its journey and what are the secrets of God. Most of us rely on the teachings of religions and care not for any personal experimentations, for the knowledge of God appears to them beyond human reach. Though, as we have said, some moments do come in the life of each individual when the spirit loaded with grief and sorrow and the mind tired and jaded, he begins to cogitate and thirst for the knowledge of God. If this feeling persists — though in a majority of cases, it does not — the awareness of God comes to him by stages. The inspiration of Scriptural books and intense desire and longing for God help him to realize God.

Occultism is a science. If it is derided as charlatanisus and fraud, it is because of the antics of its evil-doers, who alone are to be blamed not the science of Occultism. Unity in diversity is its primal teaching.

Occultism does not claim to have discovered the entire knowledge of God. As one of the Initiates has said, "We have lifted only a corner of the veil."

In search for the knowledge of the Reality, the devotee must first grasp the following fundamental tenets of all mystical and occult teachings. They are:

1) Man evolves physically and spiritually.
2) There is a great hierarchy of Intelligences called by the name of the Masters or the Elders, who direct and guide the neophtyes selected for the purpose, for speeding up the moral and spiritual progress on earth.
3) The world that is seen by the naked eye is only a small portion of the other worlds which are perceivable only by the occultists, with their inner vision.
4) The physical body is an abode of the soul, but it is not the generator of consciousness, as the biologists may assert.
5) Besides the physical body, the soul has other bodies, which are of subtler type — the astral body and the mental body, which are visible to the occultist only.
6) The whole universe is an expression of energy. All the embodied and disembodied entities are the store-houses and transmitters of this energy.
7) The Law of Cause and Effect works immutably throughout the universe. It can not be escaped, so high is the sense of Divine justice.

These fundamental tenets of occultism should be considered as so many lenses in the telescope, used by the occultist for his investigation and the realization of God, who is the supreme object of the goal of life.

We generally have a conception that the brain is the thinking organ. Cyril Scott in his book, "*An Outline of Modern Occultism*" refers to the discovery of a certain apparatus by a French scientist by the application of which it was shown that, in ordinary cases, the function of the brain could be inhibited and that in several instances, persons considered as idiots, exhibited marvellous reasoning faculties. This is a demonstration of the fact, that it is some hidden agency which is the vehicle of knowledge.

The scientist makes use of physical instruments for discovery of knowledge. The occultist has no need of such instruments. His instruments are the inward perceptions, which are latent in every man and require to be unfolded.

What is the method of unfolding inner consciousness in man? We have said, that one of the principal tenets of belief in the teaching of occultism is the law of *karma* and re-incarnation. When the physical body ceases to function and the soul passes off, it returns after its stay in the other worlds and occupies a new body. All the knowledge of its past experiences is inherent in the soul. It carries a sort of chart of all its previous recollections and experiences. The brain being a physical organ has no memory of the past. If the mind is subtlized, the soul in man, which is the store-house of all past experiences, can be tapped. The occultists regard the soul as the key to the secret doors of the universe. Just as the bottom of a lake can be seen only when ripples on its surface ceases and the waters become absolutely smooth and unruffled, the impression of the soul can be felt when the lower mind is curbed and made still by means of deep concentration, meditation and contemplation. The approach to the soul is by control of the mind.

What are the mental whirlpools that obstruct the passage to the inner-self? The feelings of anger, jealousy, hatred, resentment, malice, selfishness, religious bigotry. They not only disturb the mind butt irritate the nerves. Unless the vehicles are completely refined — made sensitive — the inward soul and its impressions would not be felt. Anything that clogs the astral and mental bodies must first be removed. Prejudices, even when they are in favour of any persons, are a form of untruth, and therefore, they corrupt the aura of the soul. A foolish mother, who fondles her child and thinks it is the best in the world, an artist who sticks to his own notion of art and will not give countenance to any other school of art, could progress spiritually. They are their own enemies. The occultist must free himself from all sorts of emotions and prejudices, if he wishes to progress. Emotions are a combination of desire and thought. Desirelessness and the control of such emotions, as lead to impatience or violence of temper, should be aimed at. Cool and serene thinking is a *sine qua non* in the life of an occultist. To take things as they come, without grumbling or complaining, and to work on in all sorts of conditions, congenial or uncongenial, are necessary. Carelessness is as undesirable as overscrupulousness.

We know the instance of John Bunyan. He was a pietist who wrote that most beautiful religious work, *The Pilgrim's Progress.* He was punctilious to such an extent, that even the most negligible points of offence appeared to him as heinous crimes and he allowed himself to suffer, under their cruel weight. He was always repenting and asking God for pardon for offences, which were most imaginary than real.

Fearlessness and courage are also essential for one who wants to tread the path of mysticism. When a man is above the average, morally and spiritually, he is always misunderstood, maligned and mis-represented. At such a time, the mystic should not ask for help but should draw his inward strength from the feeling of God within him. It is the remembrance of the Self—the Divine Being—that should instil, in the heart and mind, a joyousness, to counteract the evil effect of the mischief of maligners. Lord Buddha said, "Do not complain and cry and pray, but open your eyes and look. And it is so wonderful, so beautiful, so far beyond anything man could think of, or pray for, and it is for ever and ever."

Sorrows and losses, the result of past *karma*, must sooner or later pass away. They are not real. They should bring an inward joy of the awareness of God, before which all the earthly pleasures and enjoyments pale into insignificance. If we are only here to be channels for Divine Force, why should anything worry us or bother us. Clairvoyance and clairaudience are the faculties which mystic may develop. The spaces and sounds of the invisible worlds become known to him. He sees the planes peopled with innumerable entities. At one end of the scale there are millions of intelligences which are concerned with the growth of the mineral, plant and insect life. At the other end are nature-spirits, angels, fairies, principalities, of unimaginable beauty, working incessantly in response to the cosmic law of evolution. To a clairvoyant, thought forms are discernible and thought is the language of the universe.

"To our naked, physical eyes, the cosmic laws may appear imperfect. But viewed by an occultist, they are perfect in every respect. The Vedantic philosophers consider matter as illusory, not in the sense, that it has no existence, but that it is deceptive. In the universe there are two schemes of evolution going on side by side — the evolution of matter and the evolution of intelligence." Just as the gross body evolves, the subtle body also evolves and to the eyes of the clairvoyant the whole process of evolution, both of the form as well as of life, becomes known and visible.

The law of causation and effect does not work only on the material plane. It operates also on the subtle planes. Man is not only a trinity of spirit, soul and body, but there are some other intervening factors such as mind and emotions, which should also be taken into consideration. As St. Paul says, "There are two bodies — the spiritual and terrestrial." The physical body is the terrestrial body and the celestial bodies are the astral, mental and spiritual bodies. Just as, by exercise we develop the physical body, the subtle bodies can also be exercised and the length of time, which each of the subtle bodies will remain on the respective subtle planes, after the departure of the soul from the physical body, depends upon the way they have been handled and refined. If they are refined they become light and live for a longer time on the higher plane, after physical death. If an individual soul is darkened by the dark shades of malice, vengeance, hatred, discord, selfishness, indolence, lust, it gravitates to that part of the lower astral plane, where it finds souls of like nature. They become earthbound. They make their habitation in these regions of emotional suffering, till their coarse astral atoms are disintegrated and they rise to the higher strata. They cannot go to the mental plane to which other more refined souls can rise after a time in the astral world. The death of the soul in the astral plane means birth of the babe in the mental plane. This is how the process of birth and death goes on in the various planes of existence.

The mental plane is a superior plane, where souls enjoy a peaceful and blissful time on account of their meritorious deeds on the physical plane. The law, "As you sow, so shall you reap" works relentlessly in all the spheres and planes of life. Life is a continuous chain of births and re-births, till man achieves the goal of *nirvana* and is eventually merged with God.

The inner government of the physical world is carried on by a great Hierarchy of Adepts, spoken of by the Theosophists as members or Masters of the Great White Lodge. They have great super-normal powers. We shall speak at length on the subject, in a separate chapter.

The awareness of God, and the attainment of the knowledge of the super-physical planes, is the goal of occultism. It is not only expansion of consciousness, but an access to a state of unconditional bliss, which is the birth-right of every individual. It is his sheer foolishness and ignorance that keeps him away from such a blissful state of consciousness. And the main object of this work is to stimulate and inspire our readers to attain God-realization, which is not an impossible feat, but one within the reach of every man, if he has a determined will and intense longing for God and Truth.

Says Lord Krishna in the *Shrimad Bhagavat*: "He who is engaged in the performance of yoga, who has subdued his senses and he who has concentrated his mind on Me (Krishna) — to such *yogis*, all the *Siddhis* stand ready to serve."

Siddhis are the supernormal powers that are attained either by the occult method of self-purification, meditation, concentration or by developing psychic faculties which are inherent in some persons. These powers appear to be abnormal, because at present they are uncommon, but there is nothing unnatural about them. But these powers expose the possessor to certain dangers. The first danger is pride. Egotism is the greatest obstacle in the path of spiritual progress. If a man becomes a clairvoyant and begins to feel puffed up with the notion that he has been specially selected by God to become the founder of a new dispensation, he would be courting disaster. He would be digging his own grave. He would get into the clutches of mischievous entities who will make a sport of him and ruin him.

The second great danger is ignorance, which is much greater than pride. Man has made no study of the science and, in his ignorance, misunderstands everything. To speak in the works of Dr. Annie Besant — "He magnifies a copy book maximum into a fragment of divine wisdom, a platitude of the most ordinary type into an angelic message. Then, for want of common knowledge on scientific subjects he will often utterly misunderstand what his faculties enable him to perceive and he will in consequence gravely promulgate the present absurdities."

The third great danger is that of impurity. If a man has an impure nature and is not free from selfishness, the exercise of the psychic gift will lead him into a hopeless mess. It would mean his ruination, bodily, mentally and spiritually. But if a man be unselfish, pure in his thoughts and aspiration to serve God and mankind, any psychic gift will become an aid and an instrument in the path of God-realization.

Just as intellect is commonly found among good people and bad people, psychic gift is an acquisition of not only good people, it often happens that weak-minded persons are born with the psychic gift and in the case of such persons the development of the psychic faculties may do them more harm than good. The longest is often the shortest route and it is always advisable to develop the clairvoyant and other faculties by treading the rigid and strong path of occultism and to avoid the short cut of psychism, for it is dangerous in the case of persons, who have not developed their moral and spiritual character.

It is not surprising that Theosophists run down psychism. But whether they are wholly justified in that crusade against the science of Spiritualism, we shall consider later on.

L.W. Rogers, a student of the occult science says, "Enthusiasm is the power of God made manifest in a human being. Reading and observation are merely collecting soul food. After collecting the food, we must assimilate it in our system, by deep thinking. Quiet thought is necessary after reading. One should cultivate the aspiration to live up to the highest in him. Life rightly lived is joy. Realize that this little life is but the dull and the gloomy morning of the coming, radiant day. Look forward to the future with joy and gladness.

Each man must retire to know himself and his environment. He must obtain first-hand knowledge of the mysteries of life. He must purify the vehicle of consciousness. He must develop his spiritual powers, that he may be of the greatest possible assistance in spreading the light and helping others forward. He must calmly, and serenely, give himself up to reflection on higher life. His mental attitude should be of reception and not surrender. He should be as one who listens for the faintest whisper from the depths of being, but who uses discrimination in its testing and reason in its interpretation. He should be at all times mentally and morally awake and alert.

One of the divine characteristics of occultism is its absolute justice. Each is exactly what he makes himself and gets precisely what he earns, not a jot less nor more. He merely comes into his own. Self-reliance and resoluteness are absolutely necessary.

Unselfishness is a man's best protection. It is not facts we need so much as capacity to live, to love, to know the joy, that we are unable to comprehend. One grows most spiritually, when the life stream flows most through him to others. One who seeks to have and to hold is like a pond, without an outlet, covered with its green slime of impurity. He represents spiritual stagnation. One who receives and gives again is like a lake from which springs a noble stream to quench the thirst of parching fields beyond.

God is the only Reality. What joy, what knowledge can be deeper than that of God-realization. It is supreme bliss. The path of renunciation becomes easy as soon as man gets even a glimpse, a whispering sound of the great Reality, which is God. All the toil and moil become easy of endurance, when the mystic sight is acquired and the problem of life becomes easy of solution. The love consciousness is joy consciousness. To see God in everything is the way to self-realization. God is the sum and substance of all our ideals. He is the supreme object of the desire of our life. Religious organisations create bondage. But every man can realize truth himself, without the aid of any organised institution. His own soul holds the key. He has only to feel the impulse towards God and that something in him will take him towards the goal.

The human heart is God's abode. Is it not said in the *Katha Upanishad*, "He who entering into the heart (i.e. looks into his own heart) perceives Him abiding there, sees him (also) in all the elements. This is That which is coeval with the Breath of Life, who enters and abides in the heart."

Karl Von Eckartshansen was a German mystic of the 18th century. A most gifted writer, he has written on various subjects—his works comprise drama, politics, religion, history, art criticism and general science. He has published in all some sixty-nine works and has contributed largely to mystic and occult science also. His work, "*God is Purest Love*" is said to have run into sixty editions in Germany and it has been translated into several European languages. In common with other mystics Eckartshansen's main teaching is that within all of us, there is dormant faculty, which when developed leads into a new world of consciousness, resulting in the union of man with God, In common with others, he holds the heart to be the motivating factor in the development of this consciousness. Christ's teaching, "Love God with all thy heart and thy neighbour as thyself" has a considerable mystic significance, however common-place it may appear to be.

Eckartshansen says,"The love of God and his neighbour is the motive for the Christian's will and the essence of love itself is Jesus Christ dwelling within us." The Christ within means love in essence and attainment of wisdom which is the guiding principle of morality and reason. Wisdom and love are the two forces, that combine to rend the transcendental veil for achievement of God-realization.

It is said in the Bible, "Many are called but few are chosen." (St. Matthew ch. 22 Versa 14). It is only the few that can gain the secrets of the mysterious wisdom. It is only the eagle that can stand the dazzling light of the sun. It is only the prepared soul that can come from the outward court, which is the external temple of God into the interior of God's abode. The exterior leads to the interior, but few succeed in entering into the interior realm.

What religion is externally, mysticism is internally. Religion is mere belief, faith. Mysticism is true understanding, realization.

We shall explain the various phases and steps of the ladder, which the mystic has to climb before he can reach the final goal of union with God, in spirit and in truth in a separate chapter.

4

The Mystic and the Magician

We have explained in the foregoing chapters that the mystic's is a complete life, because he lives in God. Is there anything greater than God? Can any one desire anything more than God, on this earth or in heaven?

A learned man in search of God, was directed to see a *fakir*, at a certain place. He found him and met him.

"God give you good day" said the learned man to the humble *fakir*. The latter answered, "I never had a bad day."

"God give you good luck."

"I have never had ill-luck."

"May you be happy, but why do you answer me thus?"

"I have never been unhappy."

"Pray explain this to me, for I can not understand it."

Then the *fakir* clad in dirty rags said to him with a beaming smile "If I am hungry, I praise God; if it freezes, hails, snows, rains whether the weather is fair or foul still I praise God; if am I wretched or despised, I praise God and so I never had an evil day. You wished that God may send me luck. But I never had ill-luck, for I know how to live with God and I know that what He does is best; and what God gives me or ordains for me, be it good or ill, I take it cheerfully from God as the best that can be and I have never had ill-luck. You wished that God would make me happy. I was never unhappy; for my only desire is to live in God's will and I have so entirely yielded my will to God's that what God wills, I will."

The learned man retorted; "But if God should will to cast you into hell, what would you do then?"

"Cast me into hell? His goodness forbids. But if He did cast me into hell, I should have two arms to embrace Him. One arm is true humility, that I should lay beneath Him and be thereby united to His holy humanity. And with the right arm of love, which is united with His holy divinity I should so embrace Him, that He would have to go to hell with me. And I would rather be in hell and love God than in heaven and not have God."

The *fakir* showed to the learned man that self-surrender to the will of God in utter humility was the route to the realm of God.

The mystic understands that he comes from God and he has to go back to God. That is the goal and end of life. In the Vedas, it is taught that man descends from God and he has to ascend to God. To the mystic, the soul is his kingdom. He rules his senses inwardly and outwardly. He lives a life of ecstasy for he has no desires that bind him to the earth. His mind is always uplifted towards God. He thinks of God, he dreams of God, God dwells in his heart, every hour of his life. His soul is turned with the supernatural state. He makes the supernatural to be his natural environment. He lives in the world of spirit, not of matter. He sees all things in the universal light. He is a reservoir of spiritual energy and not a mere canal. His profound experience is "suffering in God". A man of prayer, he knows the true value of prayer. His heart, mind and soul are wrapt up in the splendour of God. He is full of the Eternal spirit. His mind is deeply rooted and grounded in the thoughts of God and in the sanctity of life. He loves God; he adores God. He worships God in silence and in perfect adoration full of love for all His creatures. His is a full life, for he is deeply engrossed in love divine.

Ignatius Loyola, the great Catholic mystic said. "I come from God, I belong to God and I am destined for God." This sums up the whole teaching of mysticism. The mystic is one who feels the transcendence of God and His immanence. He is full of joy, for when God's light falls upon him and he lives in the splendour of God, he cannot but be happy. It is said of the great mystic, Ruysbroeck, the pastor of a parish church in Brussels, that he used to walk into the streets to and fro with his mind concentrated on God. He was in this manner sending out currents of divine love for the consolation and uplift of the broken and bruised ones of humanity out of the depthness of his heart. Such is a mystic.

We are not using the word mysticism in the sense of the vapourings of the brain or a search for fanciful vision. The mysticism that we talk of has its root and centre in God. It is a most practical form of religion. To speak in the works of that great mystical writer, Evelyn Underhill:

"It (mysticism) is in its widest sense the reaching out of the soul to contact with those eternal realities which are the subject matter of religion. And the mystical life is the complete life of love and prayer which transmutes those objects of belief into living realities: love and prayer directed to God for God Himself and not for any gain for ourselves."

The mystic wields the wand of the magician. The mystic and the magician are one only with this difference that the mystical magician uses his powers for the good of mankind, but the magician, who has conquered the secrets of the supernatural world and uses the power gained for his own selfish ends and aims, is not a mystic. There is White Magic and there is Black Magic. Black Magic is sorcery. White Magic is highest Wisdom.

It must be stated definitely, that magic in its purity of motive is the highest science or wisdom, based upon knowledge and practical experience. A tree grows from a seed sown in the soil, nurtured by water and air and a child grows into a man. We consider this growth as natural in both these living organisms and it is truly so. We do not add anything externally, either to the sapling or to the child. When we build a house we have to put a stone upon a stone, a brick upon a brick and then it is completed. But it is not so in the case of living organisms. They grow because of the interactions of the inner forces. The centre of each living organism is a reservoir of energy which flows from God. What makes a tree or a child is that spirit, which is a ray of the One Life that transcends and is immanent in the whole nature.

Man is the crown of God's creation. With the spirit of God in him he can make such abundant use of that spirit, that he can transcend matter and acquire supernatural powers. "Magic is the science which deals with the mental and moral exercise over himself and others."

In order to understand the miraculous and magical power of man, we must investigate and study man's relationship with the universe. Man is a microcosm and the universe is a macrocosm. The elements that compose man are the same as in the universe. The ocean contains millions and billions of drops, but man is only one drop in that ocean.

He is but one spark in the flame. The microcosmic man and the macrocosmic nature are one.

All religious teach us that God is the Supreme First Cause and nature is the effect of its manifestation. They also teach us that the object of life is union with the First Cause. There are powers latent in man but the method of unfolding them is so difficult that very few achieve or realize the goal of life, namely, union with God. This union can become a *fait accompli* by acquiring spiritual knowledge or the knowledge of the soul. The mystic does it. The key to this spiritual knowledge or the unfoldment of the powers latent in the human soul, is the acquirement of self-knowledge. We can now understand why such great stress was put by the ancient Greeks on the formula "Know Thyself".

The Absolute Spirit in Its manifestation becomes the Trinity, the Father, the Son and the Holy Ghost working on the three different planes, — matter (earth), soul (water), and spirit (fire). Spirit, soul and matter are the three primordial elements. Spirit is compared to fire and in the Zoroastrian religion the greatest importance is given to this element. It is the creator, "the great carpenter of the universe." It is immaterial, formless and universal.

The second element is the soul which is compared to water. "It is a semi-material element, formless in its original state." It permeates in all forms and when it departs from any form, the latter perishes. For the perfection of human life, the soul has to enter into human bodies, several times. The number of its excursions into human bodies, depends upon the nature of experiences gained. When life becomes perfect, the soul ceases to re-incarnate. The soul is the house of the spirit. Between spirit and matter, there are various other grades of invisible matter and they are represented by the soul.

The third element is matter or body which is compared to earth. The invisible material element which permeates through the universe becomes condensed and takes shape "by the organising power of the soul".

These three primordial elements, Spirit, Soul and Matter, act and react upon one another and by their interaction, four intermediate links are created, thus making a septenary of seven principles.

The existence of the seven principles is spoken of in all religions. According to esoteric philosophy, the one originating cause becomes manifest in seven fold directions. The One Creator brings forth seven cosmic planetary Logos of which one is the Solar Logos of our system. This latter again emanates from seven Planetary Logos referred to in the Christian Scriptures as "the seven spirits before the throne". in the Zoroastrian Scriptures as "*Amshaspands*" and in Jewish Scriptures as "*Elohim.*" These spirits said, "Let us make man". Thus the one becomes divided into many, in order that each individual soul may evolve in matter and enjoying the blissful consciousness of the One becoming perfect, come back to the original source from whence it emanated. The same seven principles of which the universe is formed, exists in man. They should not be considered as separate for they are like the seven notes of the same octave.

Man, a unit, a trinity, enters into four states of consciousness, namely, the waking state, the dreaming state, the sleeping state and last, the most important, the consciousness of God. He may be regarded as manifestation of three higher and three lower powers and if he succeeds in allying himself with the three higher powers, subjugating the lower, the unmanifest then becomes manifest.

The human heart is the temple of God. It is the reservoir of spiritual energy. If the brain is overfed, the heart is starved. The soul depends for its nourishment not on emotions but on the power of the divine spirit within the heart. The heart is the seat of consciousness and not the brain. The consciousness of the brain is like the false light of the moon. The Consciousness which arises from the heart is the true light of the sun. Pure, unselfish love is the greatest factor in unfolding the mysteries of the universe.

We reiterate that there is no such thing as a miracle. What happens is the result of the action of law in nature, which is eternal, immutable and ever active. There is the visible nature, there is the invisible nature; the objective nature and the indwelling energy that vitalizes its growth.

Besides these two, there is a third part of nature, which is spirit, the source of all forces. This latter is eternal.

Just as nature is triune, man is also triune. He is made of body, soul and spirit. If the spirit dominates and the soul is united with the spirit, man becomes immortal.

Magic is both a science and an art. As a science, it is the knowledge of these principles, by which the omnipotence of the Spirit over the forces of nature can be gained. As an art, it is an application of this knowledge in practice.

Zoroaster was one of the first, who knew the secrets of nature and was thus sable, because of his sincerity, devotion, love, austerity and piety, to unfathom the mystery of the universe, by delving into the depths of his heart and unfolding the latent powers inherent in every man. He was called the *magi*, and the Zoroastrian religion — the first revealed religion – was called the *Magian* religion. Magic, which is derived from the word *magi* is used today in a degraded sense. But in the ancient ages, it was held as divine science, the objective of which was participation in the attributes of the Divine Self and realisation of celestial powers.

Madame Blavatsky considers Zoroaster to be the founder of magic and it is very strange that this religion, which is full of mystical knowledge, which gave birth to Gnosticism and various other religions and philosophical schools of mysticism, is today shorn of all its secret teachings and is followed by a little more than a thousand hundred persons only, who are quite content with its ethical teachings of "good thoughts, good words, good deeds," unware of its grand mysticism.

It is not only in the *Vedic* religion that you get the teaching of *yoga*, Zoroastrianism also contains the teachings of *yoga*. Christ said, to his select disciples, "To you, it is given to know the mysteries of the Kingdom of God, but to them it is not given — therefore speak I to them in parables, because they seeing, see not, and hearing they hear not, neither do they understand." (Matthew XIII 11–13)

The hidden knowledge is so dangerous that only those of determined will, purity of heart and unselfishness of purpose and devotion to God, can be benefitted thereby. It is therefore that the secrets were revealed only to the few by the founders of the various religions.

Those making good use of the divine science are White Magicians. Those who abuse it for their own nefarious ends, due to this egotism are Black Magicians.

There are in nature the Elementary Spirits — Sprits of the four elements, viz. the earth, air, fire and water, called by the Kabalists, gnomes, sylphs, salamandars and undines respectively. They are forces of nature and they can be used or employed by disembodied spirits whether pure or impure and by living adepts of magic and sorcery for good or bad purposes as they may desire. We hear of the elementary spirits in many legendry stories. Shakespeare's plays are full of these beings variously named peris, devs, djins, sylvans, satyrs, fawns, elves, dwarfs, trolls, nouns, nisses, kobolds, brownies, necks, undines, salamanders, goblins. In all ages and in all centres, they have been feared and invoked, banned and blessed.

Besides these elemental spirits, there are elementary spirits. They are disembodied souls of the most depraved character. Prior to death, having separated themselves from the divine nature they have lost their immortality. They hover in the wide span of nature and after considerable time they get themselves disintegrated and are lost. The Black Magicians contact the lower strata of the discarnate spirits. Those who enter thaumaturgically into a higher form of perception are White Magicians or Brothers of Light. They are the beloved of God. Those who enter into the lower form of perception are Suicide-Squads who destroy their own soul's victory. They are Black Magicians or Brothers of the Shadow.

It is said of a notorious vivesector and black magician, Gilles de Rays, marechal of France, better known as "Blue Beard" that in order to advance his knowledge of the arcane science, he tortured to death, one hundred and sixty women and children. What a holocaust to satisfy the lust for evil power.

It should be stated that search after arcane power or the *siddhis* as it is said in Sanskrit, is not the end of the mystical science. If the mystic or the magician does it, he will miss his divine vocation. He will misinterpret the divine voice. The true aim of the mystic is union with God through knowledge and love. Participation in the life of God is the target to be aimed at and not thaumaturgic experiments. Even celestial visions should not be encouraged, as they are signs of spiritual weakness. The highest type of magic or mysticism is to rise to God without rites and evocations.

Let us then move to the City of God or as the poet says, towards,

"The great world to light that lies,
Behind all human destinies"

It is said in the Bhagvad Gita,

"Devote thy heart on Me, worship Me, sacrifice yourself to Me, so shall thou come to Me." (IX-34)

Man is his own creator. He can convert the clay of his body, with the help of the within him, by will and wisdom into a temple of God; he can unite his will with the Supreme Will and thus become a God. This is the magic of life.

SECTION II

MYSTICISM IN WORLD RELIGIONS

5

Mysticism in Zoroastrianism

Zoroaster was the Magi sage who established the religion of Magianism, later on called Zoroastrianism in ancient Bactria, some six thousand years before Christ. Theologians and historians have not been able to trace the antiquity of this great religion to any exact date. They even say, that there was not one prophet by the name of Zoroaster or to be more precise Zarthustra, but a series of prophets, seven in all, who came to the world at different times and different places. The last is historically known as the one who flourished and established his religion in the reign of Shah Gustasp. Greek and Roman writers make plentiful references to the teachings of Zarthustra, known to them as the great Magi Sage. When the Jews returned from their Babylonian captivity, they brought the teachings of Zarthustra with them, which is a proof of the antiquity of this great religion and the influence it had upon the Greek and Jewish thought.

The Greeks hail Zarthustra as a great Initiate and look upon his religion veiled in symbols and mystical rituals as the finest and most authentic record of divine science. In fact, Zoroastrianism or Magianism was the chief source of both esoteric Judaism and esoteric

Christianity and we may even say that the initiates of the Greek Mysteries were animated to no less extent by the mystical teachings of this great sage of antiquity.

Zoroaster got the revelation like other prophets upon the top of a mountain. Communion with God, he showed was possible only after long endeavour in search of God and by leading an austere and strenuous life. Zarthustra is said to have got his revelation as a result of a life of austerity and deep meditation, on Ushidarina, a mountain by the river Daraga (*Vandidad* XLIX). Moses received the table of the Law on Mount Sinai (*Exodus* XXXIV). The Koran was revealed to Mahomed on Mount Hava. The Hindu Rishis lived in the Himalayas.

In order to understand the sublime mysticism embedded in the faith established by Zarthustra, we must refer to Greek and Roman writers, who were more aware of it, than unfortunately, our modern savants. The veiled mysticism in Zoroastrian rituals and philosophy is to-day more or less lost and the religion which was the greatest glory of antiquity followed by a very large number of its adherents is to-day in its decline followed by a little more than a hundred thousand Parsis in India and all over the world, most of whom are indifferent to it or are unaware of its unique and sublime mystic charm. The Greek writers often called Zarthustra by the name of the Assyrian "Nazareth". "Nazareth" is derived from the word "Nazar" or "Nazir" which means "set apart" or "separated". The Nazirs were a sect of very ancient Adepts known for their spiritual healing. Plato calls Zarthustra the son of Ahura Mazda, a name of the Good Principle in nature among the Chaldeans. The Magian religion was named of Machagistia and Plato considered it as "the most uncorrupted form of worship in things divine". Aristotle, Pliny, Plutarch and various other Greek and Roman writers refer to this great mystical, militant saint and seer in their works both as a prophet and a reformer—one who gave his teachings to the world in two garbs. To the masses, Zarthustra, like Christ, spoke in plain language, putting emphasis on his great ethical teaching of *Humakhata, Hukta, Huvarshta, Mansni, Gavasni, Kunasni*, which was the key and substance of the Zoroastrian exoteric teaching and to the initiated he gave the hidden secrets for acquiring the secrets of nature and thus attaining union with Ahura-Mazda, the final goal of life.

It must be remembered that though Zoroaster was called a Magian or Magician, his utterances were purely of a divine nature and the word "magic" must be understood in its original divine sense of wisdom-religion. In fact, he denounced all sorts of sorcery and the practices of incantations indulged in by daeva worshipers. By daeva worshippers is meant, devil worshippers. The Scriptures speak of Zarthustra as possessing rare spiritual powers "and living in intimate communion with divine natures". Dr. Haug says, "The few philosophical ideas which may be discovered in his saying, show that he was a great and deep thinker, who stood above his contemporaries and even the most enlightened men of many subsequent centuries."

Col. Olcott, one of the famous founders of the Theosophical Society, speaking in Bombay to an audience of Parsis said that Zarthustra knew more about nature than Tyndal, more about the law of Force than Balfour Stewart, more about the origin of species than Darwin or Hackel, more about the human mind and it potentialities than Mandaley or Bain. To the man to whom the secret of the universe is an open book, not only does the knowledge of physical laws come easy to him, but he knows much more; he knows the working of the cosmic laws, which is beyond the conception and vision of the highest intellectual scientist.

The mystical aspect of Zoroastrianism is lost to the world because most of the sacred books of this religion were destroyed by Alexander the Great and subsequently by the Mohammedans when they conquered Iran. Further more, whatever fragments are left have been translated from the original languages of Zend and Avesta by Western savants, mostly, Grammarians and it can not be expected of them to delve into the inner mysteries veiled behind symbolic teachings.

It is said by occultists that though the sacred scriptures of this great religion have been lost, there are copies lying hidden in the underground temples and libraries of occult literature and some day or the other, the glory and sublimity of this faith which once swayed the people of a large empire will be once more revealed to the world.

Zoroaster is characterised in *Yasna* as "Famous in the Aryan Home country." This gives us a clue, that Zoroastrianism must have once prevailed in India and the learned Dr. Darmesterer (Vol IV of the *Sacred Books of the East*, edited by Prof. F. Max Muller) says, in his preface to the translation of the *Vendidad*, "The key to the Avesta is not the Pahlavi, but the *Veda*". It appears that Zoroastrianism was co-eval with the religion of the *Vedas* and both Brahmanical and Zoroastrian religion, in fact, we should say that all world religions owe their origin to the same source, namely, the mighty Brotherhood of High Initiates. Madame Blavatsky speaks very highly of Zoroastrianism and refers to its occult side in both her works, "*Isis Unveiled*" and "*The Secret Doctrine*". She says, "The Western scholars may say,:

'The key to the Avesta is not Pahlavi but the *Vedas*, but the occultist's answer is — 'aye' but the key to the *Vedas* is the 'Secret Doctrine'.

There is considerable truth in the statement of Prof. Max Muller when he tells the Parsis, the present day followers of the Zoroastrian religion, that they are the "disinherited sons of Manu." Both the Zoroastrian and Vedic religions have so much of common in them, that it is obvious that the teaching of "*yoga*" which is the predominant trait of the *Vedas* must have also occupied a dominant position in the Zoroastrian system of thought. And what is *Yoga*, if not an occult teaching from the start to the finish? We are given to understand, that even before Ahura Mazda revealed Himself through Zoroaster, some of the Iranian Kings, like Hoshang, Jamshed, Ferdun, Kaikaoos, Kaikhusru, and others were all yogis of the highest type. They had become kings of the mighty Iranian Empire in succession, because of their yogic powers which were used for the good of all. These Iranian Kings were models of kingly virtues. It is an indication of the extent of Yogism, which was current even before Zarthustra, that the last of the series of the seven prophets, bearing the same name appeared on the sacred soil of Bactria, in the time of Shah Gustasp, about six thousand years before Christ.

Zoroastrianism is wrongly criticised as dualism. *Ahura Mazda*, the Living Essence, the Supreme Being, the Creator of the material worlds, Omnipotent, Omnipresent, Omniscient, Eternal, Infinite, the Absolute Spirit is the same as Brahman, the Indescribable, the Unknowable, the One without a second, Timeless, Spaceless, Formless of the *Vedas*. The two spirits of principles of good and evil emanating from *Ahura Mazda* and allegorically represented as *Spent Mainus* and *Angra Mainus* are only the two different aspects of God for the ·process of Evolution. Man has been given free choice, to work within these two poles of goodness and evil, light and darkness. If he chooses to live in darkness, it is his own fault. If he works for perfection, choosing the path of righteousness i.e. *Asha* and *Vahu Manu,* he can come back to the original source from whence he emanated. There is duality so far as man is concerned. But there is absolutely no duality in *Ahura Mazda,* who is one without a second, the Absolute Spirit, the all Being. He is the first born out of *Zavarna Akarna* Boundless Time, but by no means he is bound by Time. In *Yasna* 28, the epithet used by Zoroaster for *Ahura Mazda* is *Apaurvim* i.e. before whom there was none. He is Eternal. We have therefore in Zoroastrian teaching the foundation of a Divine unity. It may appear on superficial observation, that there is dualism in the conception of the Godhead, according to Zoroastrianism. But it is an erroneous idea. *Ahura Mazda* is Omnipotent, Perfect, All Wise. Duality is acknowledged as far as man is concerned and it is for him to decide, whether to tread the path of righteousness, however thorny and narrow it be, or the path of evil, which broad and tempting but which leads to the darkness of night and not the light of eternity. The teaching is very clear. "Be ye servant ·of *Ahura,* not of *Aheriman.*" It is purely a question of man's exercising his own free will, which is the greatest weapon placed in his hand, by *Ahura Mazda.* The will of man is the instrument that forges his destiny. *Ahura Mazda* is the "Primeval Spirit", "The Creator of the Universe", "The Loving Father," "God who is the One that always was, is and will be".

The entire fabric of the ethical system describes in Zoroastrianism is based on the essentials of a simple teaching: Good thoughts, good words, good deeds, *Manashni, gavashni, kunasni, humakta, hukta, huvarshta.* The ancients knew the tremendous potency of thought both for construction and destruction. It is the thought that is the seed of action and the channel of speech. It is an omnipotent force for good and evil as the man may wish it to be. It is a sovereign power.

Ahura Mazda is both transcendental and immanent as in the *Vedas.* The sole purpose of the universe is that man must evolve himself into perfection for union with the Supreme Spirit.

It is said in the Bible, "In the beginning was the Word, and the Word was with God and the Word was God." (St. John 1:1). The Bible also says, "We live and move and have our being in God." And the *Mahavakya* of Zoroastrian creed, *Ahunavairya* translated means.

"As is the will of the Eternal One
So through the Harmony of perfect thought
His Energy brings forth the visible world
And His power sustains the rolling Spheres!

This *Ahunavairya* is a great *mantra.* Occult science, proves the important role of sound in the universe. There cannot be an existence unless there is sound. The universe was produced by sound. Man is the culmination of existence. In him, are all the *tantras* or forces, both visible and potential. *Ahura Mazda* (the Supreme Wise) dwells in every human being. The divine spirit latent in man has to be awakened and this can be achieved by the repetition of the *Mahavakya, Ahunavairya,* in purity of heart. Is it not said in the Bible, "The pure in heart shall see God?" There is great emphasis laid in Zoroastrian scriptures upon purity of both mind and action, internally as well as externally. Purity is the seed of God-realization.

The *Ahunavairya* contains twenty one words, that is thrice seven to be heard. The number seven has an important significance in the mystical teaching of Zoroastrian lore.

There are in all seven *Amesha-spentas,* six of whom are the attributes of *Ahura Mazda* viz. Good Thought, that is divine thought, that which is "the word" in man, Excellent Holiness, Perfect Sovereignty, Divine Piety, Health and Immortality. The seventh *Amesha-Spenta* is the synthesis of the six *Amesha-Spentas* and that is *Ahura-Mazda.* There is a very significant invocation contained in *Yast* 19, verse 16. It says, "I invoke the glory of the *Amesha-Spentas* who all seven have one and the same thinking and the same speaking, one and the same doing, on and the same father and Lord-*Ahura Mazda.*" This is a clear teaching of the unity of God, in multiplicity of His forms, — the same teaching that we find in the *Vedas* as also in other religions.

We see the septenary system running throughout all the world revelations. We notice it in Christian as well as Jewish scriptures. They are also extant in the *Vedas* and the *Gathas.* The following table gives a sub-division of septenary Man as referred to in *Yasna* and in accordance to the confirmed views of occultists:

According to the occultists	*According to Yasna (Chapter 55, para 1)*
1. *Sthula Sharira* — The physical body.	1. *Tanu* — The physical body.
2. *Prana* — The vitality.	2. *Ushatana* — Heat or vitality.
3. *Linga Sharira* — The ethereal double.	3. *Kherpa* — The aerial mould in which the

	body is cast (Persian Keleb, Kalbud)
4. *Kama* — Desire, sensation, passion, emotion.	4. *Tevishi* — Out-going energy, desire, emotion, force.
5. *Manas* (i) Lower *manas* giving intelligence reason. (ii) Higher *manas* giving intuition, spiritual knowledge, holding in store the experiences of all lives and striving to become immortal by uniting with the Spirit.	5. *Urvan* — Soul, *manas*, the re-incarnating Ego, the one that suffers or enjoys.
6. *Buddhi.*	6. *Bodhang* — Intelligence, reason.
7. *Atma.*	7. *Fravashi* — Spirit, the divine principle underlying every atoms of the elemental, mineral, animal and human kingdoms.

The above is described in the *Avesta* as under: "We declare and positively make known this (that) we offer (our) entire property (which is) the body (the self, consisting of) bones, vital force, aerial form, desire, consciousness, soul and spirit to the prosperous, truth-coherent (and) pure Gathas (prayers)".

The followers of Zoroastrianism are accused of worshipping fire. They are not fire-worshippers but worshippers of *Ahura Mazda*, for fire is the greatest and sublimest symbol of God. It contains in it the hidden light — the Light of Lights, the source of all life. In the books of antiquity, this element of nature is held in the greatest reverence. The following significant passage from the writing of the great English mystic Robert Fludd, of 17th century is very enchanting.

"Regard fire, then, with other eyes than with these soul-less incurious ones, with which thou hast looked upon it as the most ordinary thing. Thou hast forgotten what it is — or rather thou hast never known. Chemists are silent about it — Philosophers talk of it as anatomists discourse of the constitution (or the parts) of the human body. . . . It is made for man and this world and it is greatly like him — that is mean, they would add, — But is this all ? Is this the sum of that casketed lamp of the human body ? — thine only body, thou un-thinking world's machine — thou man ? Or, in the fabric of this clay lamp, burneth there not a Light ? Describe that ye doctors of physics ! — Note the goings of the Fire — Think that this thing is bound up in matter chains. Think that He is outside of all things; and that thou and thy world are only the thing between: and that outside and inside are both identical, couldst thou understand the supernatural truths! Reverence Fire (for its meaning) and tremble as it — Avert thy face from it, as the Magi turned, dreading and — (as the symbol) bowed askance . . . . Wonder no longer then, if rejected so long as an idolatary, the ancient Persians and their Masters, the Magi-concluding that they saw "All" in this supernaturally magnificent element — fell down and worshipped it; making of it the visible representation of the very truest; but yet in man's speculation and in his philosophies — nay, in his commonest reason — impossible God."

Zoroastrianism can be vindicated by no other science but the occult science. It is the mystic's paradise, the occultist's treasure trough. It is no wonder that occultists and mystics like Col. Olcott, Madame Blavatsky and Dr.

Besant should have gone into such raptures over the religion of Zarthustra, whose veiled teachings are like an open book to these savants, who have an inner eye of perception.

Just as fire is held in great reverence in Zend Avesta, *agni* is held in equal reverence in the Gita also. Lord Krishna tells Arjuna, that there is God in the fire of the Altar. "I am the Fire; I am the sacrifice." The act of the *mobed* in filling the censer with fire from the sacred altar is held symbolical of imparting knowledge of divine truth to the worshippers.

If a religion is not based on the teaching of *karma* and re-incarnation, it can not be held, that it has any esoteric essence in it. Theologians and commentators have been able to discover some passages here and there which give an indication of these truths proclaimed by the great Magi. But the western scholars, who are pure Grammarians, do not give any credence or value to such interpretations. It does not however mean that Zarthustra did not preach *karma* and re-incarnation. Without these teachings, the whole theory of mystic knowledge propounded in Zoroastrianism falls to pieces. The fact is that the sacred books of *Avesta* were burnt and we have no proper guidance. Besides, before they were burnt they were known to the Greek waiters and their conviction about the authenticity of Zoroastrian occult teachings should put all doubts to rest.

In the light of mystic knowledge, *karma* and re-incarnation are inevitable and unescapable facts. Man, in his preliminary stage, is born with animal instincts and it requires a number of births to clear off the brute in him and to become human and then super-human i.e. spiritual. With each birth, the soul advances, clearing off its old debts and finally a stage is reached, when the world ceases to attract and the person feals an insatiable desire to renounce everything for the love of God, who alone is the Reality. As the soul advances higher and higher, the desire to understand its true nature and to comprehend the secrets of the universe becomes greater and greater. The keen desire for spiritual knowledge enkindles the flame within. The inner spiritual senses become keener and more active. The person takes to a life of austerity; he works for the sake of work without expectation of any return, he crushes his individuality and personality; praise or censure does not affect him; He rises above everything. He controls his thoughts, his emotions, his desires. His will become an instrument of power. His self-consciousness grows into divine knowledge. He becomes perfect and when he reaches the final state, he is well called, a *yogi*, a holy man, an adept, a *Mahatma*.

Does Zoroastrianism speak of union with *Ahura Mazda*? Our reply is definitely in the affirmative. Though we have only fragmentary material to rely upon for authorization of this conception, fortunately we have sufficient evidence in the *Yasnas* to prove this. We give below a few relevant quotations from the *Yasnas*:

"May we see Thee, attain to Thy oneness, by the best purity, the perfect purity."

— *Ha-60* (20)

"Him will we serve with praiseworthy prayers
for now is He revealed to the (inner)
eye. He who in acts and speech
and thoughts knows Purity, he (knows).

Ahura Mazda" — *Ha-8* (40)

There are several passages in the *Gathas* also composed by Zarthustra himself which indicate union with the Absolute Spirit, *Ahura Mazda*, as a final goal of life. We quote some of them as under:

"Who so, O Ahura! believe Thee as Lord by their actions, speech and good prayer, whose primitive Protector Thou art, O *Ahura Mazda*! they by the glory of their purity at last will merge in Thee".

(*Gatha Vohukhshāthrem,-Ha-51-3*)

"Every one is wise through the purity of Armaiti, all that (is) in Thy kingdom, O Ahura".

(*Gatha Spentomad-Ha-49-5*)

"Who so units swiftly unto the pure Consciousness of the Universal Mind, take their birth in the happy, abode of Mazda."

(*Gatha Ahunāvaiti-Ha-30-10*)

The above references prove the immanence of God and the practicability of union with Him in other words, "I am in all things, all things I am".

The following passage from *Gatha Ahumavati* is also suggestive of the same thought and illustrate our point:

"To Him (i.e. to the Holy man) Armaiti approached and with her came Sovereign Power, the Good Mind and Asha (the Righteous Order) and Armaiti gave *Keherpam* (form) she abiding and ever strenuous."

There is a passage in *Hoshbaum*, which also illustrates the point in view. It is as under:

Mayest Thou rule, O Ahura Mazda! in Bliss according to Thy Will, as thou wilt over the Waters, over the Trees, over all that is of the pure origin. Make that the Holy man may rule; the unholy may not rule. May the Holy man rule as he will; may the unholy disappear, driven away by the creatures of Spentamainyu, may he be conquered, not ruling as he would."

The Adept is the holy man. When he succeeds in harmonising his will with the will of Ahura Mazda, through purity, austerity, meditation and prayers, he finds Him in his heart and lives in a plane of Higher Consciousness, bathed in the waters of eternal joy, with powers added to him. Even after reaching the Adeptship there are about sixty grades of such adepts, till the very high consciousness is attained and the self is ultimately merged in the Universal Self.

As in the *Vedas*, in Zoroastrian scriptures also, admonition is given to get the training for adeptship from a *Guru*, who must be an adept himself. This is the prayer that is generally recited, when the advanced soul is in search of a guru to take him further on, on the path of adeptship:

"Give me, O Fire, son of Ahura Mazda! (One) who can instruct me what is best for me now and for ever more, concerning the best life of the Holy men (Adepts) brilliant, all glorious."

When the pupil draws nearer to the goal, he does not then need any *Guru*, for the *atman* becomes his own instructor and it takes him along.

The heart is the seat and centre of God-realization. There should be no separateness with any one in the world. Non-seperateness and purity are emphasised in Zoroastrianism as in all other religions. The short prayer of *Jasmeavounahe* is meant to impress the pledge on non-separateness and the marriage of the soul with the Spirit i.e. God, *Ahura Mazda.*

The Zoroastrian religion is a mystery. Its secrets are embedded in its rites and ceremonies which are handed down to us from time immemorial. But these ceremonies without the knowledge of the inner meanings are useless. They appear as a farrago of nonsense, a near feast for the ignorant and the gullible. The question therefore is to lift the veil, that enshrines one of the finest and noblest mysteries of the world.

The secrets of the teachings of the great Bactrian sage were known to the Greek scholars and poets. When Akbar the Great gathered together men of different faiths at his court, after studying and comparing their essential teachings, he was so much enamoured to the teachings of Zarthustra, that "he received the sacred fire and committed it to the faithful hands of Abdul Fazil, his confidential minister." He introduced also a new religious sect called Ilahi. A new era was founded on the basis of Iranian reckoning.

It is very necessary that this religion of Zarthustra which is a storehouse of ancient wisdom should be studied by adepts, all the world over, with the help of such secret scrolls and records as may be lying buried in the secret terrains of ruined temples and cupolas and the sublimity of its exalted teachings be re-vindicated to the world.

6

Egyptian Mysteries

Madame Blavatsky's contribution in revealing the depth and greatness of ancient wisdom, as contained in the religions particularly of ancient India, Iran and Egypt, to the Westerners may be considered as *unique.* She says in *Isis Unveiled*, "The day is approaching fast when the world will receive proofs that only ancient religions were in harmony with nature and ancient science embraced all that can be known." In her books, "*The Secret Doctrine*", "*Isis Unveiled*" and "*The Voice of the Silence*", there are innumerable revelations of the secrets long kept, books long forgotten, histories of "papyri and parchments of inestimable importance" buried under the debris of ancient cave temples and ruined halls and sanctuaries. She speaks of "buried crypts, tablets and pillars, whose sculptured revelations will stagger theologians and confound scientists."

Lewis Spencer in his book, "*The Mysteries of Egypt*" says, "No land can lay claim to such a chronicle of mystical and occult thought as Egypt, the mother of magic. Herself a mystery, she brought forth the mysteries, laying the foundations of arcane science and philosophy for the future and seeming thus like some dark cavern of issue and origin, whence have emerged those shadowy sorceries and that philosophy of the higher wisdom which have proved the amazement of the succeeding ages."

(Introductory—page 18).

In the ancient world, Egypt was a citadel of the mystic science. Its sacred secrets were guarded by its priests, who were as learned, as they were pure in mind and heart. They were called initiates. They were the masters of the temples, the inner apartment of which were accessible only to the few elect. Though centuries have rolled away, Egypt's mystic charm seems still to hold sway on us. There is some uniqueness in its sacred monuments and relics. What appeals to us the most is the statue of the Sphinx carved out by the priests, the symbolic representation of Egyptian mysteries. It is supposed to represent nature, "calm and redoubtable in its mystery". It has the head of a man, bulging out from the body of a bull, with the claws of a lion and with eagles on both the sides. But however, fantastic and absurd, it may appear to an idle on-looker, it has a deep significance in it. It is symbolic of nature, representing terrestrial Isis and depicting the emergence of man from the lower animal nature. The bull, the lion, the eagle and the man in the arcane science represent the four elements of nature — water, air, earth and fire. They constitute both the microcosm and the macrocosm. Darwin discovered his theory of evolution in the 18th century, but both physical and spiritual evolution of man was known to the ancients, long, long before him. Darwin stopped only at the physical evolution of man But the ancients, knew much more viz. that man having descended from God, the Supreme Being, must by a series of births, again ascend to the God-head and be finally merged in Him.

In the Egyptian history of religion and philosophy, no name shines with such lustre as that of Hermes. His philosophy attracted the attention of the Greek scholars and they laid the foundation of Greek Mysteries, after the fashion of true Hermatic teachings. Hermes was idolised by them. They called him, "The Scribe of Truth," "The Lord of the Divine Words" and so forth. They gave him even the epithet of *Trismegistus*, meaning "Thrice Great".

Hermes taught that God was beyond human conception. He was eternal, indefinable, formless, invisible. But however beyond human comprehension, some elect persons could rise above material concerns and acquire the power to perceive the radiance of His perfection. When this is realized the initiate feels a thrill of delight, indescribable.

Hermes taught the totality of things. Whatever he saw, realized and understood, he had a power to reveal and manifest. But he concealed his writings and he gave his secrets only to select few, who were required to take a solemn oath not to divulge them to others and if they did they were put to death. Such was the severity of punishment dealt out to those who violated the secret rules and such was the strictness with which the mysteries were kept a close secret in the secret chambers of the temples and in the hearts of the Initiates.

The Book of the Dead is considered to be one of the finest contributions to the religious literature of the Egyptians. It is a compilation of prayers for the dead. The following appeal to the Initiates, from this book will be read with interest:

"Blind soul: Arm thyself with the torch of mysteries and in the night of earth shall thou uncover thy luminous Double, thy celestial Soul. Follow this divine guide and let him be thy genius, for he holds the key of thy lives both past and to come."

The Egyptian mysteries taught that when man trains his triple nature namely physical, moral and intellectual by the simultaneous exercise of his will, reasoning and intuition, he acquires supernormal powers and perceives the unseen forces hidden in nature. By prodigious efforts he can lift nature's veil and get direct perception, which opens out to him a new world and a new heaven. One who conquers self, can conquer even the most mysterious forces of nature. He becomes a seer, a prophet, a creator of souls.

Let us cast a glance at an Egyptian occult sanctuary. There is a statue of the goddess of Isis, at the entrance door seated in a prayerful attitude, with a closed book on her knee and at the foot of the engraved figure are the words written as under:

"My veil no mortal hand hath raised."

This is a challenge to the initiate to unveil the secrets of nature and become united with the Supreme Being — the kernel and upshot of the whole Hermatic teaching.

There are two columns in the temple — one is red representing the ascending spirit and the other black symbolising matter imprisoning spirit. There is an outer court yard where the candidate, yearning to get the knowledge of the mysteries is first taken. He stays here for about a week and spends his time in preparation for the adventurous journey of the spirit which he wants to embark upon. He prays and mediates and occupies his time in doing humble tasks. He is then taken into the inner chamber, by an attendant of the temple. He is warned of the great risks. If he is strong, he might succeed in finding liberation. If he is weak, he is told, he would be buried in the dark labyrinths of the dungeons. He passes through the inner chamber, where there are rows of statues with human bodies and heads of animals and serpents. At the end of the sinister chamber, there is a mummy and a human skeleton. The atmosphere is gloomy and dark, fearsome and awe-inspiring. The attendant once more gives him a chance to retrace his steps, as the journey is so fraught with danger and so few come out successful. If the candidate still persists, the attendant then leaves him to his fate. He gives him a lamp and asks him to go into the interior Hall.

As soon as he gets in this hall, he hears a voice, saying, "Here perish all who foolishly covet knowledge and power." These words are repeated seven times. The candidate takes courage in both hands and goes forward. He sees a shaft with an iron hole and an iron ladder. There is terrible darkness all round. The candidate catches hold of the flickering lamp nervously. The soul is in his mouth. There is no chance of his retracing his steps from that awful dome of blackness. If he slips, he must fall headlong into a abysmal darkness. But he goes on and on. He sees at last a place of safety. He lands himself on a gallery. There he meets a magician, who congratulates him on his passing the first test. He explains to him the meaning of the various symbols with which the walls of the hall are decorated. There are twenty-two such symbols representing the first twenty-two letters of the alphabet of the arcane science which are supposed to be the keys, which when applied give to the neophyte the power over occult forces — true wisdom and knowledge of the principles of life divine. The magician, after explaining to him the mystery of all the letters and the numbers takes him "from Isis Urania to the chariot of Osiris", and finally to the crown of the *Magi*. "Learn what this crown means," says the Master to the pupil. "Every will which unites itself to God to work justice and show forth truth enters into participation of the divine power over beings and things, the eternal recompense of freed spirits." The pupil gets a faint glimpse of the truth. He is covered with feelings of mingled delight and fear. He listens to the master's voice in subdued silence. He feels, he has touched the dawn of divine remembrance.

But the tests are not over. he is taken to another long and narrow vault, at the end of which he sees tongues of fire shooting upwards. "This is sure death" cries the pupil. The Master says. "It is not death". The pupil forces his way through the fire. The fire melts and disappears. But the trials are not over. As soon as he escapes from the crucible of fire, he comes to a lake of black stagnant water. He shivers but he plunges into the dirty water. He crosses it and when he comes out at the other end, he is attended by two persons. His wet body is dried and he is anointed. He is given a new dress and taken to a garden for rest. He recalls to memory all the pictures and images seen by him. He remembers the vision of the arcanum.

There is a wheel, which is suspended on its axle, by two columns, representing the genius of good and the genius of evil. The former has a beautiful face of a young ardent man, the latter has his head plunged into abyssmal darkness. And between the two columns is seated a sphinx, on the summit of the wheel, holding a sword in her claw.

There is sweet music in the garden. The neophyte tired, closes his eyes but when he re-opens them, he sees a most lovely form, bending over him. He does not know whether to tremble or to rejoice. The enchantress plies her trade, "Are thou afraid of me, handsome stranger?

I bring thee the victor's reward, oblivion of pain and sorrow, the goblet of happiness." This is the last and most crucial trial. If he fails he becomes the slave of the temple. If he dashes the goblet to the ground and escapes from the enchanting embrace of the "nude", he is taken to the sanctuary of Isis, clad in purple and initiated.

The apprenticeship of the initiate now commences. He passes many years in the study of various sciences. He leads a life of renunciation. He subjects himself to hard discipline. If he makes right use of the knowledge, he paves the way to the higher stages of initiation. If he in a moment of egotism, boasts of his achievements, he seeks imprisonment and he is lost.

The neophyte asks the question: "Shall I some day be permitted to seek the rose of Isis and see the light of Osiris." The reply given is "That does not depend upon us. Truth is not given. It is found in oneself or not found at all. We can not make an adept of thee, thou must become one thyself. Long does the lotus press upwards, beneath the surface of the steam, before spreading out its petals to the light. Hasten not the unfolding of the divine flower. If it is to come, it will come in its due season. Work and pray."

The neophite prays: "Oh Isis, since my soul is nothing but a tear of thine eyes, grant that it may fall like dew on other souls and that when I die, I may feel their perfume ascending to thee. I am ready for the sacrifice."

When he becomes ready for the sacrifice, his silent prayer is heard and the Master says to him: "My son, the hour draws nigh when the truth shall be revealed to thee. Already thou hast divined it by descending into the depths of thy own nature and finding divine life therein. Thou art about to enter into the mighty, ineffable communion of the initiates, for thou art worthy by thy purity of heart, by love of truth and power of self-abnegation. No one however crosses the threshold of Osiris, without passing through death and resurrection"

The neophite becomes an adept.

There is enforcement of silence in all mystical teachings of the ancients, and in Egyptian mysteries the Sphinx stands for the symbol of silence. Another symbol of great significance is the serpent head, representing the goddess Isis. The serpent among the ancients was venerated as symbolising spiritual wisdom. This we find not only among the Egyptians but among the Hindus of the *Vedic* times also. The teaching of the serpent power is called *Kundalani* in Hindu scriptures. Madame Blavatsky says in her great occult book, "*The Voice of The Silence*:"

"In silence we worship God.
Who desires to worship God's majesty
In truth, he must plunge himself into the secret silence."

The voice of the ego is the voice of the silence. When senses are conquered and personality is suppressed, the ego gets a free play and the mystic hears the voice not only of the soul but also of the spirit, of the nirvanic plane. It is then that the spheres above begin to speak and the mystic feels the joyousness of God, — the "Eternal Bridegroom of the Universe." He looks into the infinitude of time and space. He hears the songs of the constellation and the voices of the numbers. The knowledge of God, His Oneness and the unity of the life, dawns upon him. He sees in the vast vistas of nature, the same law operating everywhere, above or below, in the vast span of the sky or the microscopic cave of the human heart.

Knowledge, purity, faith, silence, — these are the potent weapons the mystic wields in conquering the secrets of nature and attaining union with God, the crowning glory of every human soul, that has to take a number of births in human bodies to achieve the diadem.

In the Egyptian Mysteries, considerable importance is given to the ritual of re-births. It is not the object of this book, to describe in any detail the rites and ceremonies observed in the Egyptian temples and mystic schools. But it must be said that the religious rites were performed only with a view to bring about purification of the mind and creating thoughts of hallowedness Lewis Spencer in his beautiful work, *The Mysteries of Egypt* devotes a whole chapter to the subject at the end of the book, and after giving description of all the various types of rites and ceremonies that were observed in ancient Egyptian Temples and in Greek and other Mysteries, he says, "The externals of initiation constitute merely the portals of the true knowledge of the spirit. Ritual of itself is naught compared with this knowledge any more than 'table manners' are in respect of eating. These symbolize the process and lend dignity to it and that is all. Rite and symbol apart from high intention and spiritual significance, can even be degrading, yet though often express much more than mere words are capable of expressing, that is, they are efficacious as supplementing the imperfect medium of human speech in the conveyance of subliminal ideas, although they must not be regarded as actually achieving any act which will have magical or supernatural repercussions upon the spirit of the initiate."

What is the philosophy and the purpose of the whole initiation? Let us summarise it.

The man who wants to be initiated is brought as if it were in a chamber of new consciousness. He goes through three stages in the path of initiation. The first is of purification. The rites and ceremonies are supposed to lift his mind and heart to something that is not mundane. Thus purified, he is taught concentration and this concentration in return brings illumination. Initiation is an inward act of the soul. It all depends upon the psychic power of the initiate and his own inward feelings, towards the sacred teachings. The teachings of the certainty of God, his goodness and graciousness and certainty of man's union with the divine spirit,—the ascent of the soul after its descent into matter—give a hallowed significance, if the initiate's heart get in tune with the sacredness of the atmosphere created by the Mysteries.

Writing on the ancient mysteries, particularly of Egypt and Greece (we shall refer to Greek Mysteries in a subsequent chapter), Lewis Spencer pays a most eloquent tribute to this ancient wisdom. It is worthwhile quoting the whole passage as it has such a pleasant ring about it, that it may find its echo in the heart of the reader:

"Magic and the true magic is, indeed, the very heart of the philosophy of the Mysteries. The life is mystical, the way is mystical, as are the life and way of magic, the Magic of enchantment of that "unreal" which is more real to the mystic than the real, of that ecstasy which is the higher music of the universe, that rapture which is translation and life in the divine. The true poet, who is invariably a mystic—who cleaves to that higher and lofty apprehension which beggars "thought", and the mystic, who must after all be a poet, penetrates these realms to the confusion, jealousy and dismay of lesser men simply because they hold the "sesame" to rapture which the world seeks through the betinselled and shoddy pageantry of pleasure instead of in the vast tapestries of spiritual space and in those sphery heights that are the true abiding places of the soul of man.

For what is there to learn in this apprenticeship of life other than the essential poise and approach to Otherwhere? This world is indeed an aerodrome in which man is building, fitting and testing these winged pinnacles which shall bear him to immortality. If he fail in his 'prentice task — then must be assuredly return to the scene of his toil. The process is wrongly described as of the nature of punishment or retribution. It is merely the self-discipline of the Divine endeavouring, at great distances, to justify itself by various experiments in the depths of time and space, sending out its colonist particles to replenish the spheres to triumph ere they return to the Fatherland and gain new strength from the sources of the Ultimate."

We now thus understand the significance of Mysteries. Its teaching is to harken man, to leave off the shibboleths of material life, to refuse to play the pantominic part in the drama of human life and to enter into the inner world of consciousness, which must lead to higher and higher stages of ecstatic joy, as he approaches to the final goal of God-realization. The purpose of initiation is to realize man's place in the divine scheme of existence and the Egyptian Mystical system, the oldest in the world, has shown how this could be achieved, in an orderly manner, stepping from mortality to immortality, from consciousness to higher consciousness and from higher consciousness to the joy, its rhapsody and the ecstasy of union with the Infinite.

7

Mysticism in the Vedas

The grandest mysteries are enshrined in the ancient Vedic Scriptures. The *Bhagvad Gita* is one of the most sublime mystical scripts. The scholars have not still been able to find out, which is the more ancient religion — Vedism or Zoroastranism, or whether the two were brother and sister religions which flourished at the same time but later on, on account of religious frictions caused by man made dogmas, the two parted company, one section departing to Iran and the other stabilising itself in India, the seat of hoary tradition, and the land of the highest *rishis* the world has ever produced. The close resemblance in the two religions is due to the close resemblance between the Rig-Vedic Sanskrit and Avesta languages and the sameness of their mystical teachings.

The word "*Veda*" comes from the Sanscrit "*Vid*" to know. And the word "*Avesta*" is also derived from the Sanskrit word "*Vid*" to know. It is not our purpose here to enter into any controversy regarding the identification of Vedism with Zoroastrianism. We have dealt with this subject in our book "*Oneness with God*". What we wish to point out is that the main object of the religions founded in ancient times was knowledge. Faith is certainly the foundation of all religions, but it should not rest there. Religion is supposed to give us not mere faith in God but also knowledge of God.

Vedism is a highly mystical teaching. By its practice the hunger of the heart can be satisfied and the devotee can get the real experience of God. The goal of life can be achieved even in this bodily existence.

The mystical way is the safest way to the Kingdom of God. It is by love, devotion, control of the senses, unselfish service, purity, and austerity that one can enter into the Kingdom of God. Lord Krishna says to Arjuna in the *Bhagvad Gita*, "But this love is not for those who can not control themselves, who do not worship Me and who will not hear My voice. Nor is it for stubborn ones and blasphemers. He who reveals this mystery of all mysteries to those who worship Me, who at the same time sacrifices to Me the best of all works, will surely come to Me. There is nobody else who could render Me a better work than such an one. Also none will be dearer to Me by sacrificing his knowledge. This is My commandment. He who accepts this love with faith and without blaspheming shall enter the realm of the blessed without hindrance." (*Bhagvad Gita Chapter III-67*).

The *Vedas* speak of four kinds of Yoga — *Karma Yoga, Bhakti Yoga, Gnan Yoga* and *Raja Yoga*. The last Raja Yoga is the crown of all Yogas. The devotee may take any of the paths or all the paths to reach *Brahman*. What is required is the detachment of the mind from earthly desires and possessions and keen concentration on the Supreme Being, "If anyone thinks constantly of Me he will verily come to Me" (Bhagvad Gita). We have written at considerable length on all the four *margas*, — *Bhakti, Karma, Gnan* & *Raja Yoga* — in our book,

Oneness with God, and we do not want to reiterate the teachings of these yogas in this work.

Thought is concentrated force, and devotion is a great factor in the evlution of life. There is a conception prevalent that *Vedism* is a pessimistic religion that imposes a teaching of non-action. In the case of the highly advanced *sanyasis*, their attitude of non-action should not be despised for as we have said in the foregoing pages, a detached cloistered life of silence has a considerable value in the economy of the world. Thoughts of saints and sages are vibrations and they radiate joy and create a new world though the creators of such a new world are unknown to us. But for the majority of people a life of activity is a *sine qua non* for the progress of their souls. The Bhagvad Gita therefore lays a great stress upon the importance of *Karma Yoga*. It teaches *Nishkama* that is work without expectation of any return or reward. The following extract from the *Bhagvad Gita*, — the Lord's Song is very important:

"Be unselfish, subdue your sense and passions which obscure reason and lead to deceit. Low men follow examples, great men give them. The soul ought to free itself from the bonds of action and act absolutely according to its divine origin. There is but one God and all other *devatas* are inferior and mere forms (powers) of Brahma or of Myself. Worship by deeds predominates over that of contemplation."

We have shown in our book, *Oneness with God* that the essential teachings of all religions are the same. They all speak of the unity of God, the physical and spiritual evolution of man, *Karma*, Free Will, Re-incarnation, the principles of good and evil in life and man's ultimate goal of life namely his union with God. God is the Supreme Being, both transcendent and immanent in nature. Madame Blavatsky speaking of the superiority of the ancient sages over modern scientists says in her memorabe work. *Isis Unveiled*, as under:

"The modern or the so-called exact science holds to a one-sided physical evolution, prudently avoiding and ignoring the higher or spiritual evolution, which would force our contemporaries to confess the superiority of the ancient philosophers over themselves. The ancient sages ascending to the unknowable made their starting point from the first manifestation of the unseen, the unavoidable, and from a strict logical reasoning, the absolutely necessary creative Being. Evolution began with them from pure spirit. which descending lower and lower assumed at least a visible and comprehensive form and became matter. Arrived at this point, they speculated in the Darwinian method but on a far more large and comprehensive basis.

Rig Veda-Samhita is considered to be the oldest book of the world. It is said in this book:

"Not-Being and Being are in the highest heaven in the birth place of Daksha, in the lap of Aditi."

"In the first age of the gods, being (the comprehensible Deity) was born from Not-Being (whom no intellect can comprehend); after it were born the Regions (the invisible) from them Uttanapadas."

"From Uttanapadas the Earth was born, the Regions (those that are visible) were born from the Earth. Daksha was born of Aditi and Aditi from Daksha."

Madame Blavatsky explains that *Aditi* is the Infinite and Daksha is *Daksha-pitrah*, the father of gods, or rather father of strength. Daksha born of *Aditi* and *Aditi* born of *Daksha*, means co-relation of forces. The spirit descends from God and enters into matter and its, function is after countless revolutions and evolutions to ascend back and reach the region of its origin namely Brahma, the absolute.

In all ancient religions. *Agni*, fire is given the highest place of importance. It is recognised as the source of all beings, the father of strength. In the Vedas, *Akasha*, in its liberal sense means "sky" but in the language of the mystic, it means "the reservoir of all energy and propeller of every change". It is either. It is also known as astral light. It is *amma mundi*, the workshop of nature. In occult science, it is considered to be the means of realizing every quality of the spirit. It is sidereal light, spoken of in the Hermatic philosophy. It is occult electricity and in Modern Spiritualism it is the psychic fluid or force by means of which the medium contacts the discarnate spirits.

According to the *Vedas*, the Deity in the shape of ether, pervades all things. The following extract from *Katha Upanishad* gives a very beautiful picture of how the absolute Spirit makes itself manifest in its multiple forms and how man can obtain the revelation of the Absolute:

"The One Ruler who is the inner-self of all beings makes His one-form appear as manifold. . . . This is that by which all form, flavour, scent, sound, feeling and attraction are cognised even as the Self. This is That the Spirit which was before the creation of the world. — He who entering into the heart (that is, looks into his own heart) perceives Him abiding there sees Him also) in all the elements. This is That which is co-eval with the Breath of Life, who enters and abides — in the heart — And again This is That, the Omniscient, from whose Breath of Life, the sun is created and into which it is eventually absorbed again. Verily, there is none greater than He. Higher than the manifested universe is the unmanifested and higher than that is the pure spirit;

than which there is nothing more subtle. This is the hidden and unrevealed Self in all beings, which is not manifest to the ordinary sight but only by means of the Higher Sight, possessed by men of subtle vision.

"This Self is not revealed by many explanations nor apprehended by much teachings but he who is self-controlled and concentrated and steadfast obtains illumination."

Patanjali in his *Sutras* gives the key of attaining mastery over the physicial forces. He shows that God can be realized by various methods — by austerity and purity of character, detachment, self-control, concentration, meditation and contemplation. We have dealt with this subject in our book, *Oneness with God.* Spirit is diffused everywhere and the Absolute can be revealed to us only if we follow and practice the rules laid down by Patanjali in his *Sutras.* Madame Blavatsky in her work, "Isis Unveiled" (Vol. 1) says:

"Spirit is the medium of magnetism. Magnetism consists in the imperial will of man. It is not the spirit of heaven and hell which are the masters of physical nature but the soul and spirit of man which are concealed in him as the fire is concealed in the flint."

Before man can get a glimpse of the Divine Spirit, it is necessary that he should pay off his past debts. Everyone is born with certain *Karma*, the result of his past incarnation. Karma should not be confounded with Fate. Fate presupposes an angry God who wants to take vengeance on an individual by sentencing him to a certain span of life's suffering. This is not really the case. The suffering in life is the outcome of man's lapses in past lives. The Law of *Karma* is the most beneficent law of God. It is a law of adjustment. The Bible says, "As a man sows, so shall he reap". This is, in fact, the teaching of all religions. It is not only individuals that make *karma* but even nations make karma. Why have such mightly empires as the Roman, Greek, Persian, Babylonian, Spanish and now British have fallen? Because of the *karmas* of the nations concerned.

The first requisite then for the aspirant for God's illumination is paying off his past debt's. When these are paid off, he starts with a clean slate and thus purified he can get God-realization if he persists in his endeavours. Every man has been endowed with free will. This free will is the imperial power in his hands. He can make the best use of it and pave the way to the ultimate goal.

Madame Blavatsky says, "The Law of *Karma* operates on all planes, save that of the pure spirit. From the occult point of view progress and payment of past debts are closely related. As debts prove a hindrance to man even in the world of commerce, so also in the domain of spiritual evolution."

When we are born, the soul retains the recollection of past lives. It carries a chart of all past experiences. But man does not get any consciousness of the past, because brain is the physical part of the human body and that being a new vehicle, there is no continuity as in the case of the soul.

> Madame Blavatsky says in "The Voice of the Silence."
> "The mind is the great slayer of the Real.
> Let the disciple slay the *slayer.*"

There is a depth of meaning in the above line, namely, that "The mind is the great slayer of the Real". Mind is the sixth sense, nay, the king of the five senses. Just as we require the five senses to be suppressed for the realization of God, the distractions of the mind also have to be overcome. By mind, what is meant is the lower mind, that which is veiled in matter, the *kama-manas*, the *chitta*. Restraining the whirlpools of *chitta*, the lower mind is the objective of yoga, as taught by Patanjali in his *Yoga Sutras*. This lower mind works like a monkey and to curb it, is essential for spiritual progress. The mind in its fullest sense is called by Shankracharya and other Vedantists *Antah Karana*. It is composed of four parts, — the I — (*ahankara*); insight, intuition or pure reason (*buddhi*): thought (*manas*) and last discrimination of objects (*chitta*). Now chitta is the lower mind and thought (*manas*) is the higher mind. It is the lower mind that has to be slain to allow the triad of the theosophists, viz, *Atma-buddhi* — manas, to triumph. The lower mind is the personality, which is a great obstacle in the path of spiritual progress. If a man were to see as Dr. Besant says, with "lifesight" and not "matter sight" he would climb the ladder of spiritual life and attain perfection. In this path of progress all likes and dislikes have to be overcome; all prejudices and fixed habits have to be avoided; fears and desires have to be dropped. We have to do the will of the Higher Self, even give our life for it, if needs be. It is in this way that we shall cease to hear the many and discern the One, which is the goal of life's journey. All delusions disappear. We see the bright light of haarmony, peace and progress and get the sense of inward delight at the perception of the unity of God, who alone is Real.

The Vedic Scriptures speak of the Serpent fire as the *Kundalini*. When it is awakened man obtains super-consciousness. The serpent in the Bible is described as a devil. In Hindu and Egyptain scriptures it is an emblem of health. It stands for man's healing power. It is also an emblem of immortality according to the Vedic teachings.

As we have explained in *Oneness with God* there are two nervous structures in the human body—(1) the cerebro-spinal through which the conscious mind is expressed, (2) the sympathetic system consisting of a number of nerve centres on each side of the spinal column from one end to the other end of the spine.

The *Chakras*, which is a Sanskrit word for the vortices of energy are situated within the etheric double. They are as links between the physical and higher bodies. They are placed on the right as well as on the left side of the spinal column. They form a magnetic field for the electric current to flow when the serpent fire, which lies dormant at the base of the spine is awakened. This force lies coiled up like a snake and it can be successfully aroused by means of certain breathing exercises and by concentration, meditation and contemplation. There are three channels called in Sanskrit, *nadis* through which the serpent fire flows. They are (1) the central spinal column- *Sushumna* (2) *Ida*, which is situated on the left side of the spinal column and (3) *Pingala*, which is on the right side. The *chakras* are

(1) *Mooladhara* : the root chakra
(2) *Swathistana* : the chakra near the spleen
(3) *Manipura* : the chakra near the naval
(4) *Anahata* : the chakra in the region of the heart
(5) *Vishuddha* : the throat chakra
(6) *Ajna* : the chakra between two eyes
(7) *Sahasvara* : The crown chakra.

When the serpent fire flows through the various chakras, it transports men into higher and higher regions, as it sweeps and goes upwards. The various divine qualities of man are unfolded and his perception and powers increase. When the serpent fire touches the last chakra, the devotee attains union with God. The Pituitary body and the Pineal Gland are the seats of spiritual power. They are situated in the brain. When the serpent fire contacts *Ajna* the spiritual sight is awakened. It is the "Key of David". The dovotee gets perception of Truth. It gives him *nirvana* i.e. liberation from the cycle of births and deaths. When the serpent reaches the last chakra viz *Sahasvara*, the Pineal Gland which is called the third eye is opened and the devotee gets complete rulership of all the faculties. It is union with the Supreme.

Says Krishna in *Shrimad Bhagivat-Gita*,

"He who is engaged in the performance of Yoga, who has subdued his senses and who has concentrated his mind in Me (Krishna), such Yogis all the Siddhis stand ready to serve."

The *Siddhis* are the extraordinary or abnormal powers which are attained by the practice of yoga. It must be remembered that there is nothing unnatural in the obtainment of such powers. They are in fact, quite natural powers but so very few realize them, that we call them abnormal. It must also be noted that only those who are absolutely pure and disinterested and have unnselfish motives must strive for them. In fact, the obtainment of *Siddhis* should not be the goal. They are attained with very little effort when union with God is the sole object and noting else. Is it not said in the Bible, "But seek ye first the Kingdom of God and His righteousness and all these things shall be added upto you."

Unfortunately, instead of taking the longer route to home, people go in for short cuts which are full of danger and they bring themselves to grief and trouble.

A man may be born with certain psychic gifts, such as clairvoyance and clairaudience. These gifts are the result of his good *karma* in the past life, but they might prove dangerous to him, if he does not take precautions and change his mode of life and thinking. Pride, ignorance and impurity are worst enemies. It often happens that a psychic gets elated if he becomes a clairaudient or a clairyoyant and he may thinks that he is some superb being whom God Almighty has chosen for the revelation of His message. He would be courting disaster if any such foolish notion gets into his mind. Mischievous spirits would make a tool of him and ruin him, for self-conceit is considered to be the greatest danger in the path of progress. Besides, it must be remembered that the astral sense and the mental sense of both hearing and seeing may lead him into the lower worlds and if he has not the power to resist, he may be undone. He will be inflicted with sights and sounds of an undesirable type which may distraught his mind and cripple his mental activity. Such are the dangers of possessing psychic gifts, if not properly understood and used. But these gits are of invaluable help if the psychic devotes his attention upon loftiness of character and is actuated with the sincerest motives of doing good to all mankind, without a thought for himself. Perfection of character, unselfishness of motive and knowledge of the scriptures — these are *sine qua non* in the path of spiritual progress.

The *siddhis* can also be obtained by means of drugs. *Soma juice* is considered as very holy in the Scriptures of Hindus. By its use, some sort of powers can be obtained but it is most injurious and dangerous. Such injudicious methods should be kept at a distance.

Mantras, it is said, also help in gaining a consciousness of the higher regions. The significant word in the Vedic Scriptures is *Aum.* The repetition of *mantras* at the time of ceremonies or in the quietness of pensive hour, with mind fixed upon God and in an utter feeling of humility and detachment is helpful.

Another mode of awakening the inner consciousness is considered to be the practice of austerities not excluding mortification of the flesh. There is no doubt that they have some value in developing one's will power. But *hatha yoga* has very little of spiritual value. Of what avail is it keeping a hand aloft till it withers and dies away? Of what avail is it a yogi burying himself in a pit and coming out alive after some time. Sleeping on a bed of nails, till the flesh is pierced and the body becomes a bundle of dripping blood may cause awe and admiration but of what avail are such barbarous practices. They are in fact unspiritual. For God wants us all to be happy and joyous. He does not want us to harm our body. For the body is after all the temple of the soul. It should not be pampered at all but at the same time it should not be injured and crippled.

In the *Bhagvad Gita* Lord Krishna says:

"The men who perform severe austerities, which are not prescribed by the scriptures, wedded to vanity and egotism, impelled by the force of their desires and passions, unintelligent, tormenting the aggregated elements which form the body and Me also, seated in the inner body — know these are asuric in their resolves."

(Chapter XVI — 17 & 18)

What are the real *tapas* so necessary for spiritual life? Says Lord Krishna in the Gita: "Reverence to the gods, the elders, the teachers, and the wise, purity, straight forwardness, continence, and harmlessness are the *tapas* of the body; speech, truthful, pleasant and beneficial and the study of the sacred words are the *tapas* of speech; cheerfulness, balance, silence, self-control and being true to oneself are the tapas of the mind." (Discourse XVII — 14, 15, 16)

Dharana, dhyana and *Samadhi* are highly spoken of in the Vedas. Translated in English, these Sanskrit words mean, concentration, meditation and contemplation, respectively. Truly speaking, there is not much of difference in these words for all of them nearly mean the same, though in the Vedic literature they mark different stages of development. The faculties and powers which they cause are the eight *Siddhis* described as under:

(1) *anima*, the power to become as small as an atom.
(2) *machima*, the power to become as large as a giant.
(3) *laghima*, the power to become as light as straw or cotton.
(4) *garima*, the power to become as dense and heavy as iron.
(5) *prapti*, the power of reaching out as far as even the moon.
(6) *prakamya*, the will power to realize all wishes and desires.
(7) *ishatwa*, the power to control and to create.
(8) *vashitwa*, the power of command over all objects.

The story of Lord Krishna and the Gopis has a deep occult significance. The story runs as under:

The gopis are bathing in a lake and Lord Krishna a child of six years, is sitting on the branch of a tree playing his flute. He sees the clothes of the Gopis on the embankment and quietly hides them. The Gopis were unware of Lord Krishna's presence when they had discarded their clothes and had entered into the waters for bathing. But when they want to come out, their eyes fall upon Him and they feel ashamed and find themselves into a predicament. Their clothes are also missing.

Lord Krishna then administers to them a rebuke and tells them that as they have sinned, they must expiate for their sin by coming out and taking the clothes from His hands. They come out, get back their clothes and worship Him.

The occult significance of the story is, that when a person is on the path of Initiation, he or she will have to face many dangers and trials. At the last stage of the Initiation, when the darkest hour approaches, which must eventually lead to the dawn of God-realization, it is necessary to strip oneself of everything. The soul must be purified of all earthly attractions. Naked it had come and naked it must go. In the last stage of the ordeal, one should not invoke the aid of any one; not even of his guru, but submit himself or herself completely to the will of God. It is only when this is done that the soul attains the consciousness of Brahma — *Sat Chit Ananda.* Complete detachment and submission to the will of God form the main teaching of the Vedic mysticism.

Dean Ingle says,"The mystics are the morning stars of the race, pioneers in an unchartered land "They" can crowd eternity in an hour or stretch an hour into eternity. Such powers were those of the ancient *rishis* of India, particularly. India still continues to be a land of *sadhus* and *fakirs,* mystics and saints. To those who can hear the melody of the spheres and feel the divine presence in their hearts, the attractions of the world have no hold over them.

8

Mysticism in the Bible

When we study the Life of Jesus Christ and his teachings in the Bible especially in the four gospels and the epistles of St. Paul, which may be considered as the fifth gospel, Christ appears to us in the three-fold capacity of an Indian Yogi, a Zoroastrian Magi and an Egyptian Adept. His divinity was proclaimed and this aroused the jealousy and hatred of the Jews, who persecuted him and eventually succeeded in getting him crucified. His followers consider him to be the only Son of God. But Christ never laid any claim that he was the only Son of God. He said, "I and my Father are One". This is true. But it must be also remembered that he always said also, "Ye are all gods. I am Thou and Thou art I and where thou art, there am I also and in all things am I sown. And from wheresoever thou gatherest Me, in gathering Me thou gatherest thyself."

The teaching of the atonement of Christ is unfortunately wrongly interpreted by the Church. If we look with the occult eyes certainly Christ took birth in the human flesh for the salvation of mankind. The very word Jesus derived from the Hebrew word, Jehoshua, Jeshua or Joshua, means "Jekovah is salvation." His teachings, if followed, would give salvation but it does not mean that those who are born in the Christian faith alone can get salvation by the intercession of Christ. The Christ has to be re-born in man. What is meant is that man by forcing his will has to rise to the highest in him and become perfect as Christ was perfect and it is only then, without the aid or intercession of any one that he can become one with God. Every man is potentially a god. He has to exercise his imperial will and climb the ladder of spirituality following faithfully the commandments of Christ and lead a life of abstinence and purity, with the mind fixed on God and the heart engrossed in the love of all mankind. It is by this path of Initiation which Christ like other yogis and adepts in different countries, treated, that the liberation of the soul can be attained.

Man is the creator of his own destiny. Is it not said in the Bible:

> "Though Christ in Bethlehem a thousand times be born
> If he is not born in thee, thy soul is still lorn."

In all the "Bibles of Humanity", in the *Vedas* and *Upanishads* of the Hindus, in the *Tripitaka* of the Buddhists, in the *Zend Avesta* of the Parsis, in the *Koran* of the Mohammadans and the Old and New Testaments of the Jews and Christians, there are common teachings. The same truths are declared over and over again in different terms and different garbs in all the religions. These are:

(1) God in One. He is the Creative Spirit.
(2) Life is one. There is no separateness. Separateness is a delusion.

(3) Man is spirit, entering into matter to gain experience.
(4) In the beginning, he is unaware of his divinity and falls a prey to temptations, which bring him bitter experiences and sufferings.
(5) He unfolds his latent powers as he progresses from incarnation to incarnation and ultimately becomes divine.
(6) The steps in the ladder of spiritual evolution are service and sacrifice, renunciation and resignation to the will of God.

Outwardly, the Bible is a collection of historical facts, mixed with philosophy, prophecy, law, poetry and exhortation. But inwardly, it comprises a grand teaching, the teaching of the evolution of the soul and its marriage with spirit i.e. man's union with God, which is the goal of life.

In the Christian Bible, water is symbolical of the soul. The soul has a dual aspect. It is pulled by two different forces in opposit directions — the spirit from above and matter from below. In the early stages of evolution, matter has a greater attraction and the soul gets embedded in material things. It goes through a round of suffering and when it is purified by bitter experience and penances, it allies itself with spirit.

It is impossible for a soul to get purification in one birth. It took aeons of years for the soul to tranmigrate from the mineral to the vegetable and from the vegetable to the animal kingdom and it must take several incarnations for the soul to become perfect in the human body. It all depends upon man's own individual efforts.

The repudiation of Christ's teaching of *karma* and re-incarnation by the Christian Church is erroneous. There is plenty of evidence in the gospels, especially, in St.

John's which of all the four gospels is the most mystical, as it comprises occult truths. Take the following quotations from the Bible:

"Master who did sin, this man or his parents, that he was born blind." Jesus said, "Neither hath this (blind physical) man sinned nor his parents, but that the works of God should be made manifest in him." (St. John, Chapter IX verse 2)

"Except he be born again, he can not see the Kingdom of God." (St. John, Chapter III verse 3)

"Marvel not that I said unto thee ye must be born again. (St. John Chapter III verse 7)

"That which is born of flesh is flesh and that which is born of spirit is spirit." (St. John III verse 6)

The expression "neither can they die any more", implies that they had already died and more than once.

Jesus gave his teachings to the people in two different ways. To the masses he spoke in parables. He knew that they were not capable of understanding the deeper significance of life and he therefore resorted to the method of teaching them simple truths in a simple manner. The deeper truths regarding Cosmic Laws, the involution and evolution of the soul and the ultimate destiny of man were revealed only to the select few, chiefly his apostles. The secrets of the universe were taught by him to the select initiates only. Christ had learned the secrets of Egyptian Mysteries. He was acquainted with powers of Indian Yogism. In fact a god himself, he was born with all the sacred powers over the forces of nature, which he exercised when necessary, not to vendicate his superiority but out of human feelings to help those in distress. He subdued the storm in the waters of Galilee to pacify the frightened crowd of his disciples who were crossing the lake in a boat with him. He healed lepers out of compassion. He cured various incurable diseases out of pure love and sympathy. When Lazarus died and Mary and Martha cried bitterly, Christ to assuage their grief, raised Lázarus alive from his grave where he had lain for full four days. To resurrect dead bodies to life is a miraculous power of the highest extent and this Christ exercised not to vindicate his divinity but out of sense of deep love and sympathy for human suffering. When at a feast, the wine was short and the host was in a predicament, Christ turned the water jars into wine goblets. When there was no food, he gave a feast to hundreds and thousands out of a few grains of corn.

Christ gave his secret teachings only to the few. He is said "Unto you it is given to know the mysteries of the Kingdom of God, but unto them that are without all these things are done in parables."

Christ did the miracles because he was a *yogi.* He was pure, chaste, spotless, self-sufficient, humble to the core, the lover of all, — high or low, rich or poor, virtuous or sinner. Unostentatiousness, forgiveness, freedom from egotism and vanity were the landmarks of his soul. Detached in mind, he went about from place to place spreading his message of love. His heart was fixed on God — His Father and he prayed, meditated and contemplated ever and anon, whenever he was alone wrapped up in nature's solitude and silence. Spiritual wisdom obtained from a state of superconsciousness was his crown.

The Indian yogi says, "I am Brahman. I am He" and Christ likewise said, "I and my Father are One." He chose as his immediate followers those who were pure in heart and poor in spirit. Mary and Martha, Peter, John and Paul were some of his most devoted followers.

God is love; God is joy. Christ devoted every minute of his life to spread the joyousness of God all around. He led a strenuous life relieving distress, curing diseases, preaching the word of God, creating a new phase, a new hope and revelation in the minds and hearts of hundreds and thousands and millions of people, who followed him from place to place and to all of whom he was a loving father, a generous giver.

He is invited by a Pharisee to a feast. He is received without any warmth of heart. A fallen woman, Mary Magdalen, by name, "weary in soul and sick in body" comes in. The Pharisee upbraids her for coming near Christ. But Jesus allows her to do what she likes. She kneels down and taking out fragrant oils from her bag applies them on the feet of Jesus. The latter turning his face to his host says: "When I entered in thine house, as thy guest, thou gavest me no kiss, yet this woman, since the moment she came in was held my feet with tears and wiped them with her hair; thou gavest me no kiss, yet this woman since the moment she came in has hardly ceased to kiss my feet; nor didst thou anoint my head, yet this woman has given me her precious balsam to anoint even my feet. And so I say, her sins which were many, are forgiven, for she has loved much.

"Love is the highest of all virtues and needs but directing into the right channels. Nay how can one love God, who has no love in his or her heart. And how can any one feel the bliss of God, if he is devoid of feeling altogether. And how can love and feeling be directed to higher channels if they have no existence whatsoever in the heart. I tell you that harlot is far nearer to the kingdom of God than the most righteous Pharisee, if he is cold and calculating and utterly without love. It is from the heart that spiritual understanding rises and not from the brain." (*The Adept of Galilee* by Cyril Scott, page 207)

The loving words of Jesus had an immediate effect upon Mary Magdalen. She changed life and became a pious devotee of Christ. She was initiated into the secrets of the science of the soul.

Christ meets a woman, a Samaritan at a well and she gives him water out of that well to quench his thirst. The latter in return gives her "living water". He looks at her clairvoyantly and tells her whole life story, which bewilders her and makes her fall at once at his feet in awe and admiration. Jesus says to her: "Lady, believe me the hour approaches in the life of every one when he shall neither worship the Divine Father on the mountains nor in Jerusalem but within his own soul. Liberation is alone for those who are circumscribed in heart. Those who truly understand worship, commune with the Divine Father in their own spirit as Absolute Being and truth. For, God seeketh such for his worshippers. He is Spirit and above all, through all and in all. Those who worship Him must do so as Spirit and in Spirit for He is the nearest of the near, the One Reality, the One Truth, the Absolute Pure." (*The Adept of Galilee* by Cyril Scott, page 228)

The grace of God was manifested when Christ made use of those memorable words: "Come into Me all ye that are heavy laden and in travail and I will give you rest."

No man can become a lover of God in the true sense of the word, unless he renounces earthly attachments. We notice his vigorous impeachment and contempt of the rich in the following words: "It is easier for a camel to go through the eye of a needle than for a rich man to enter into the Kingdom of God." (St. Matthew, Chapter XIX-24)

The two great commandments of Jesus are:

(1) "The Lord, our God is One and thou shalt love the Lord, thy God with all thy heart and all thy soul and all thy mind and all thy strength.
(2) Thou shalt love thy neighbour as thyself."

A wealty young man came to Christ and told him that he had followed all his commandments but he had still not got the vision of God. The characteristic reply of Christ was. "If thou wilt be perfect, go and sell that thou hast, and give to the poor, and thou shalt have treasure in heaven: and come and follow me." (St Matthew, XIX-21)

This, the young man could not do. To get the vision of God, it is essential, not only to be pure and lofty-minded but to acquire detachment of mind. Earthly possessions create distraction. Mystics are made of harder stuff. Happiness and illumination come only to those who are lonely and unworldly. "They shall inherit the earth and delight themselves in the abundance of peace."

Speaking in allegorical language Adam represents the whole process of creation. Eve is the soul separated from God; Mary is the soul in the process of re-absorption in God. In the Vedic religion *prana* is given a very high place. It is the creative energy. The various forces in nature, such as gravitation, electricity, heat, light and also mental forces such as mind, intellect, thought are but the menifestation of the creative energy—*prana*.

In the Bible, Abel stands for breath, vapour life, spirit. His brother Cain is an embodiment of outer life — love for possession, which kills or destroys the inner life. Woman is allegorically described in the Bible, first as the daughter of God, then as spouse of God, then again as mother of God and finally she becomes One with God. In this allegorical picture we have the history of the soul, which descends originally from the fountain and Source of all Life — God — enters into matter, suffers and gets experience, grows and develops and finally it is merged in God.

There was no such thing as the immaculate conception of Mary when Jesus was born. If such a miracle had happened, it would have been a violation of the law of nature. The facts are Joseph the carpenter and Mary his wife, belonged to the Essenian Brotherhood which enjoined upon its members the vow of absolute continence. They both developed the faculty of clairvoyance. It is said that the Spirit Gabriel came to both Mary and Joseph and left a message to them both, that, in spite of their vow to keep chastity, they must provide a body for the birth of a highly evolved soul, who would be the Saviour of the world. They were compelled under the circumstances to come together in purity of mind and thought to give effect to the command. This is how Jesus was born in absolute purity but certainly it was not a miracle.

The Bible like all other religious scriptures contains esoteric teachings regarding the involution and evolution of the soul. The soul descends from God, with all the attributes of the Deity latent in it. As it enters into the matter, the struggle against material possessions and desires starts resulting in its banishment from the Garden of Eden. It goes into wilderness. It at length returns and is united with God. This redemption, atonement, which every human being at some stage or the other must attain.

There are three processes by which the spirit unfolds itself. The first is illumination represented in the Bible by Abraham. It is the life of faith, the belief in God and the Other World. The second stage is that of purgation. The soul tussels between the two diametrically opposite forces — good and evil — virtue and sin. This stage is represented by David in the Bible. He was subjected to extremes of experiences, higly spiritual and at the same time highly degrading. The third and final stage is Divine Union, which we find in Christ, the Messiah. The object of all mystical teachings is to so evolve ourselves as to beome finally a Krishna, Zoroaster, a Buddha, a Christ.

The word "Initiation" is derived from the two roots "in" means into and "it" meaning "to go" that is the soul has to go or enter into something new. It is a spiritual adventure, the goal of which is union of the soul with the spirit in man i.e., God-realization.

As Goethe says in his "*Faust*",

"Two spirits dwell within the breast,
And struggle there for undivided reign
One to the earth with a passionate desire
And closely cleaving senses still adheres
Above the mist the other doth aspire
With sacred vehemence, to pure spheres."

It is said that John the Baptist, when he saw Jesus passing on the banks of the Jordan said, "Behold the Lamb of God which taketh away the sin of the world." (St. John I–25) It was he who first proclaimed Christ as the Messiah. The word "lamb" in the above expression signifies "suffering in innocence". And this is the lot of all those initiates who wish to tread the narrow path that leadeth to the Kingdom of God. The great beauty of

Christ is that he led the poor man's life in utter selflessness.

He knew that his teaching of God's truth would bring upon him a tempest of opposition and hard trials. And so it really happend. Accusations were heaped upon him. The Pharisees and the Saducees, whom Christ had exposed as hypocrites and conventionalists, burning with rage and anger accused Christ of blasphemy, for proclaiming himself as Son of God and for violating the sacredness of Sabath.

At the last Supper, Christ washes the feet of all his apostles to teach them a lesson in humility, by his superconscious powers he comes to know of Judas betraying him for thirty silver pieces and drops a hint of it. Christ is arrested. We need not dwell upon the closing scene of His crucifixion. Every schoolboy knows it. Pilate tries to avoid giving his judgment. He knows that Jesus is quite innocent. But he is over-ruled by the frenzied cries of the rabble and he orders his crucifixion.

Jesus is crucified but he rises from the grave, as foretold by him to his disciples, on the third day. For full forty days he makes his appearance at different places to different persons to convince the world of his divinity.

When Christ was crucified, it is said he cried in despair: "O God why hast Thou forsaken me." A Son of God who had borne such a lot patiently, knowing his relationship with the Divinity would have on the contrary accepted his martyrdom with cheer and gladness. Some writers think that the words put in the mouth of Jesus are incorrect. Possibly he may have uttered these words instead of what are attributed to him: "My God, How dost Thou glorify Me?" The Bible was written originally in Greek and it is very likely that the translators or the copyists may have made a blunder and interpreted wrongly Furthermore, Christ being a Yogi, he knew that he could expel the soul from his body, at will. There was therefore no necessity to apprehend any physical torture or pain, when he was put to drink the potion that was given to him for causing unconsciousness before death, which gives a greater support to the theory of the occultists that Christ must have gone quite cheerfully to the scaffold and thanked God for His glorification. His appearance in flesh after his death further testifies to His yogic powers, which were practised by *Rishis* in ancient India. Students of Vedantic philosophy and religion know that Shankacharya, one of the greatest *rishis* of India had that yogic power of separating his soul from his living body and returning to it after some time.

The following is a picture of a yogi, as given by Lord Krishna:

"He who hates none, who is the friend of all, who is merciful to all, who has nothing of his own, who is free from egoism, who is even minded in pain and pleasure, who is forbearing, who is always satisfied, who works always in *yoga*, whose self has become controlled, whose will is firm, whose mind and intellect are given up unto Me, such a one is My beloved *Bhakta*. From whom comes no disturbance, who can not be disturbed by others, who is free from joy, fear and anxiety, such a one is My Beloved. He who does not depend upon anything, who is pure and active, who does not care whether good comes or evil and never becomes miserable, who has given up all efforts for himself, who is the same in praise or in blame, with a silent thoughtful mind, blessed with what little come his way, homeless, for the whole world is his home and who is steady in his ideas, such a one is My beloved *Bhakta*." (*Bhagvad Gita*, Chapter XIV, verses 18 and 19)

The above picture applies to Christ in all repects. He was a Yogi of Yogis, a teacher of Yogins, a man of transcendental knowledge and vertues, a god in man. When he said "Father and I are one," what he meant was that the universe and the individual are one. Not that Christ alone was the Son of God but that the whole creation was the son of God. God is pure Spirit. Creation is the manifestation of that Absolute, Supreme Spirit, There is only One Life, One Intelligence, One Power, One Substance, One Spirit, One Love and each one of us is like a pearl threaded on a string, which runs through all of us. God is the current of electricity: we are the electric bulbs, which get their energy from that Fountain,—the Absolute Spirit. All is One.

There is no night in the other worlds it is all day there. Time is a human conception. Our goal should be eternity. The teachings of various prophets were based on their own personal experiences. Swami Vivekananda said, "The teachers all saw God; They all saw their own souls: they saw their future: they saw their eternity and what they saw they preached."

The mystics of all religions have laid the greatest stress upon unity of life and Christ was one of the greatest Mystical teachers. How beautifully has the poet said:

"One cosmic brotherhood
One universal god
One source, one sway
One Law beholding us
One Life enfolding us
In love always.

Anger, resentment, hate
Long made us desolate,
Their reign is done.

Race, colour, creed and caste
Fade in the dreary past,
Man awakens to learn at last
All Life is ONE."

When Jesus said "Follow My teaching", what he meant by His teaching was simply this that God being Absolute Spirit and the universe, a child of that Spirit, every being has the latent spirit of God in him. Each one of us has to become a god, a Christ, for that is the path of evolution that God has chalked out for all of us. Each individual is a ray that emerges from the Spiritual Sun. God is the Cosmic Soul, the Universal Soul, the Over-Soul; each one of us is an individual soul. The soul carries a chart of life, in which are recorded the experiences of all past lives, which help the pilgrim soul in finding its way to the destined goal of its journey.

When Christ said. "He that will, let him take of this water of life freely" (Revelation 22:17), he meant the water of immortality — the same truth — which we find in the *Bhagwad Gita*. Says Lord Krishna:-

"Within thyself thou hast a sublime friend, thou knowest not. God dwells within all men though few know how to find Him. The man who sacrifices his desires and walks to the Being who is the principle of all things and by whom the universe has been formed, attains to perfection by such sacrifice. For, he who has found within himself his happiness, joy and light is one with God. Know then that the soul who has found God is freed from old age, from death and from re-birth; such a soul drinks from the waters of immortality."

9

Mysticism in Buddhism

Christ was born in a stable and he worked as a carpenter in his father's workshop for a number of years, before the people came to know him as the Messiah. Buddha was born not with a golden but a diamond spoon in his mouth. His father was a *Rajah* in Nepal. He was born about six hundred years before Christ. He was brought up in the lap of luxury. He married a beautiful princess and had a son.

Christ was a sinless man. He was born with psychic and yogic powers of transcendental nature. He preached only for a few years and his career was brought to an untimely end by the fury of the ignorant who crucified this god-man in their frenzy.

Buddha's life, in the early years was that of an ordinary man, subject to the pleasures of the senses. But with a flash, wisdom dawned upon him and he left the palace in search of truth. He saw so much of pain and suffering, decay, and old age, that his mind was filled with sorrow and he wanted to find a solution — whether man's suffering could be ended. Just as a flower painted on a piece of paper can not emit its fragrance, but one must go to the flower itself to breath it. Buddha realised that he must find out the solution of life's problem himself by his own experimentations.

Buddha led a life of austerity and penance for seven long years. He got so emaciated that one day when he was bathing in the river, he had not the strength to resist the force of the waters and was on the point of being drowned. Sacrifices and penances, rambling in the jungles and forests all alone, without food and water for several days — all the hard *tapas* did not however give him any knowledge. But one day, meditating under the Bow tree, he got enlightenment. This enlightenment was the consequence of his great love and compassion for the suffering of all humanity. His soul was full of pity, "for the sickness of this world" and he was longing to heal it, "if healing may be found."

Buddha's enlightenment gave him the key to the mystery of the secrets of nature. He realized, "There is hope for man only in man". It was man himself who was the cause of his own suffering. He discovered or rather re-discovered the Law of Cause and Effect. He discovered the working of the *Karma*. He saw in a trance the working of re-incarnation. He found out the cause of sorrow and he also found out how that cause of sorrow could be removed. He chalked out the path which all initiates must tread if they wish to free themselves from the bondage of birth and death. His medicine to escape from the misery of life was the teaching of the eightfold path which he prescribed namely, right thinking, right speech, right aspiration, right action, right living, right exertion, right recollection and right meditation. He founded the order of the Yellow Robe and those who joined his monastry were made to take the vow of renunciation.

Buddha's name is associated with the word and teaching of *Nirvana.* What does this Buddhistic term mean? It is variously defined. One writer gives a very beautiful picture of *nirvana* in the following lines:

"The happy seat; the excellent eternal place of bliss where there is no more death, neither decay; the end of suffering; the home of peace; the other side of the ocean of existence; the shore of salvation; the harbour of refuge; the medium for escape from all evil; the transcendent, formless, tranquil state; the Truth, the Infinite, the Unspeakable, the Eternal."

Buddha taught how to achieve *nirvana* namely, by self-conquest and universal charity, by mental culture and not mental death and in order that the goal may be reached quicker he showed the necessity of forsaking the world, as the best means of gaining spiritual freedom.

Buddha has been accused of atheism. He does not really speak of God, as a Transcendental or Immanent Being. But he certainly was aware of the Absolute Spirit. His sole object of search was solution to the problem of human suffering and when he found that out, he concentrated his attention on that alone and nothing else mattered to him. The world was a snare, a *maya*, a delusion, a seat of anguish and pain. His sole motive and reasoning was therefore to stop the wheel of birth and death and he feverishly desired that each and every person should strive for *nirvana*— "the drop slipping into the ocean."

When a man reaches the extreme state of spirituality, he attains *nirvana.* Sinnet describes "*Nirvana*" as "a sublime state of conscious rest in Omniscience." It is not annihilation or extinction of the soul as some foolishly believe. It is the most important step in the path of Initiation leading from Arhatship to Adeptship.

Buddha became an Adept though still in flesh but his sense of sacrifice and his love for mankind was so great that even when he got his freedom, liberation, he preferred to serve the people for the rest of his life and even when he died, his desire was that he may be given a birth again to teach mankind how to abstain from evil and earn *nirvana*, the reward of perfect life. The keynote of Buddha's greatness is his extraordinary sacrifice and desire to serve mankind till the very last man attains his salvation. A.P. Sinnet pays a glowing tribute to Buddha for his great renunciation in the following glorious terms:

"Buddha's renunciation was in some inexplicable manner greater again, because he not merely returned from *nirvana* for duty's sake, to finish the earth life in which he was engaged as Guatama Buddha, but when all the claims of duty had been fully satisfied and his right of passage into Nirvana for incalculable aeons entirely earned under the most enlarged view of his early mission, he gave up that reward or rather postponed it for and indefinite period to undertake a supererogatory series of incarnations for the sake of humanity at large."

(*Esoteric Buddhism*, page 199)

When Buddha died, his last words to his disciples were:

"Beloved mendicants, if you revere my memory, love all the disciples as you love me and my doctrines."

"That which causes life, causes also decay and death. Never forget this, let your minds be filled with truth."

Buddhism is one of the finest ethical religions of the world. Buddha made a short shrift of ceremonies and rites. In his teaching there is no trace of all those obnoxious features which latter on entered into Hinduism and corrupted it. Buddha framed his code to suit his philosophy of attaining *nirvana* as quickly as possible. His heart burned for others' sufferings.

"I see, I feel
The vastness of the agony of the earth,
The vainess of the joys, the mockery
Of all its best, the anguish of its worst;
Since pleasures end in pain and youth in age,
And love in loss and life in hateful death,
Men to their wheel again to whirl the round
Of false delights and woes that are not false."

Born a Hindu, Buddha emphasised the fundamentals of the Vedic religion, discarding the trappings of rituals, falsely created by the priestly hierarchy to establish their own sway upon the masses. His direct and simple teaching was: "Be your own guide; be your own torch."

Buddhism places great importance on meditation. It is the secret key for unlocking the door of nature's treasure and unfolding the mysteries of the Kingdom of the Soul. It releases inner powers. It awakens divinity latent in us. The power of meditation is much greater than the energy contained in the atomic bomb.

"Your path may be clouded, uncertain your goal,
Lead on, for the orbit is fixed for your soul.
Although it may lead through the darkness of night,
The torch of the builder will give you new light.
You were and you will know, just what you are,
Your spirit has travelled, both long and afar.
It came from the source, to the source it returns,
The spark that was kindled, eternally burns.
From body to body, your spirit moves on,
It seeks a new form, when the old one is gone
And the form that it finds, is the fabric you wrought

On the loom of your mind, by the fibre of thought.
Sometime, on the same planet, somewhere and somehow,
Your life will reflect, all the thoughts of you — now,
The way is unerring, no blood can atone,
The structure you build, you must live it alone.
You are your own devil, you are your own God,
You fashion the path, your footsteps must trod,
And no one can save you from error or sin,
Unless you hearken to the spirit within."

10

Greek Mysteries

We have shown in one of the preceding chapters, the distinguished place held by Egypt as the citadel of ancient arcane science. Lewis Spencer says. "The place of the Egyptian Mysteries in the secret tradition is precise and distinct. In them was gathered up and made manifest all the wisdom and arcane knowledge of the ancient world, which was crystallized and systematized in such a manner that had it been preserved in an unadulterated form, would most assuredly have saved later ages from many religious catastrophes and much false mysticism."

These words ring too true. We know what rivers of blood were shed, all in the name of religion. The true aspect of religion not having been properly grasped, men in their bigotry forgot its essence and the Inquisition in Europe made a mockery of God. What a reign of horror and chaos it created, is a fact too well known in history.

When Egypt fell and its civilization was washed off, its priests, the custodians of the secret divine science fled to different countries and it is presumed that the Greek Mysteries were the off-springs of such exiles from Egypt. There is considerable resemblance in the Greek Mysteries and the Egyptian Mysteries. The predominant note in Egyptian Mysteries is that of unity in the universe. In fact, most of the ancient religions place a stress on this fundamental truth. God is One but his manisfestations are many.

The Greeks believed in many gods. Their love for art and beauty was astounding. Those who have an eye for beauty are generally highly strung people with impulses to do good to others. Beauty generates goodness of heart and when these two unite, the love of truth, which is a divine trait in man is created. Plato's category of the Ideal was the conception of triad, of the True, the Good, and the Beautiful. He pictured these three virtues — Truth, Beauty and Goodness, as the rays emerging from a central Sun and becoming united, returning to the Centre — the Divine Creator, the Source of all Light, Love and Beauty.

The Greeks believed in many deities and they offered in their temples sacrificial rites to appease and please them. They also had the cognizance of the Divine Spirit ruling all the deities but their temples gave them no assurance or convincing proof of the life hereafter. This gap was however filled in by the Greek Mysteries which became the most popular institution in Greece and played a very important role in the life of its people.

The Grecians had a vague conception that souls were like starry sheaves of sparks thrown from above, on earth. The Greek Mysteries galvanized the people into a definite channel of thought that the soul emanated from God and that they returned back to their original source after many births and deaths.

Pindar speaking of the beneficent, educative value of the Mysteries, says,

"Happy he who passes through the Mysteries,
He knows the origin and end of life."

In the history of the Lesser and Greater Mysteries of Greece, three persons are recognised as the greatest builders of the arcane science. They are Orpheus, Pythagoras and Plato. Orpheus is hailed as the initiate of the dawn, Phythagoras as the initiate of the full day light and Plato as the initiate of setting sun in the history of Greek Mysticism.

Orpheus was a singer. His name is associated with many legendary stories. He used to play on the flute in such a divine fashion that all nature as if it were listened to his music. It is said that when his wife Eurydice died, he felt so grieved, that he went after her to Hades and played on the instrument in such a thrilling manner that the gods of the dead were silenced and he escaped with her. Of course, this story is legendary, but it portrays the depth of his feeling and his mastery over music.

But Orpheus is known more for his religious conviction than for his music. He started what are called Orphic Mysteries, wherein the secrets of the arcane science were taught to the initiates. There is a close resemblance between the teaching of Orpheus and Pythagoras of which we shall speak later on. Orpheus prescribed abstemious practices both in food and clothing, as necessary for approach to the Divinity.

The Elusinian Mysteries which existed in different parts of Greece were more popular. They were nominally open to all citizens except murderers and such other criminals but the tribunals of the temples encouraged only those who were fit for initiation and were anxious to get divine knowledge.

The object of the Mysteries being first to create enthusiasm, elaborate arrangements used to be made in the outer court, to train the eye for beauty and the ear for music, by exhibition of works of art and by entertainment of religious songs and dancing. The votaries also participated in sacred rites and ceremonies. When they entered the inner chamber they were allowed to touch and kiss the sacred articles, symbolical of various divine truths. The votaries observed strict silence and this added to the solemnity and sincerity of the whole drama. The Mysteries had a great educative effect and they played an important role in moulding character.

All the religions have two sides — the external and the internal, the exoteric and the esoteric. The external is meant for the average mind. By external is meant popular worship in churches and temples, including rituals, creeds and dogmas. By internal mystery is meant the teaching of the occult science, the profundity of which could be understood by the select few only. The Greek Mysteries contained the esoteric teachings but not without the outer forms of religious ceremonies and rituals so necessary for training the mind and awakening consciousness in the preliminary state of preparation for ultimate realization.

At the Temple of Delphi was hung the following inscription:

"Know thyself and thou wilt know the universe and the Gods."

Our scientists about a hundred years ago — intellectual giants like August Comte and Herbert Spencer — thought that the domain of science was the external universe. They studied external nature with the aid of physical senses and implements. To them the material world was the object of their immediate concern. They ignored the knowledge of the soul. They ignored that the soul was the key of the universe. But truth was quite different to the ancients. The sages and philosopers of Greece knew the value of physical science, no doubt but they also knew that it was incomplete without the internal knowledge of the soul. They therefore investigated the possibilities of the indwelling spirit and discovered the key to the secrets of nature. Truth was inaccessible to the layman, still imperfect in charcter but to the sage, the secrets of the universe were open as a book or a mirror. The initiates in the Grecian Mysteries were gods in human flesh, whether they belonged to the Orphic Mysteries or the *Elusinian* Mysteries. The essential teaching of these Mysteries may be formulated as under:

God, which is the absolute Spirit, is the only Reality. Matter is an expression or manifestation of that Spirit but it is ever changing and ephemeral. It is the dynamism of Spirit in space and time. Just as life is eternal, creation is also eternal. Man is a microcosm, universe the macrocosm. The same laws that apply to the universe, apply to man also. To speak in the words of Edward Schure "The microcosm man is by reason of his three-fold constitution (spirit, soul and body) the image and mirror of the macrocosm universe (divine, human and natural world) itself the product of the ineffable God, the Absolute Spirit which is in its nature, Father, Mother, Son (essence, substance, life). It is for this reason that man in the image of God can become his living word. Gnosis or the rational mysticism of all times is the act of finding God in oneself by developing the occult depths and latent powers of consciousness. When that soul becomes conscious of its divinity it goes back to its original source, God. *Karma* and reincarnation are the unescapable teachings of the occult science, practised by the Greek Mysteries also. It should not be surprising if we affirm that the Greek and Egypt Mysteries together with the wisdom of the Magi of Iran and the Rishis of India, formed the cradle of the teachings of the later religions, such as Christianity, Islam and Sikhism.

The redemption of soul, which features so commonly in all religions was taught by the Greeks, in their Mysteries, in the form of an allegory known as that of Amor and Psyche. Psyche is the word in Greek for human soul. She enjoys the embraces of her divine lover in sleep. She feels His presence and hears His voice in her heart. Her intuition which is greater than reason helps her in this dreamy state of bliss. But one day, not satisfied with this vague realization, she lights the lamp of reason, and tries to locate the object of her love. To her dismay, her lover disappears completely. She no longer enjoys those early states of beatitude. She gives up the search through the channel of intellect and sensuous perceptions. Her mind is full of love for the Beloved and eventually her love triumphs. God is love and what He wants from us is, to love Him whole-heartedly and solely and not to reason about Him. Intellectual qualities are of no avail in unveiling the secrets of nature or God. Is it not said in the Bible,"Blessed are the pure in heart, for they shall see God" (Mathew V-8) The popular Indian saying is, "Purity of mind alone sees God."

Pythagoras was one of the greatest sages of Greece. He had travelled a lot and had imbibed his knowledge by coming in contact with Egyptian hyerophants, Indian Rishis and Iranian Magis. He got a vision of divine knowledge and he worked out the details by making strenuous researches in the archieves of ancient wisdom. A sage and a seer, he was able to obtain a complete and most satisfying solution to the riddle of life. He saw in a vision the triple nature of man and the triple nature of the universe. He discoverd that in the synthesis of the three worlds — the natural, the human and the divine, lay the secret of the cosmos. He found out that the cosmos was ruled by God, who was immanent in nature. He saw the inter-relationship of the microcosm and the macrocosm. He saw the ascending and the descending order of things. He saw that in the drama of universal life, the invisible were animating the visible world, that man could evolve into perfection through various stages of physical incarnations and finally attain union with the Divine Deity. He saw in the science of numbers, the key to the gates of the universe.

Pythagoras learned the theory of transmigration of the souls from the Indian sages and it became the basis of his religio-philosophy. He taught to his disciples that each existence was the reward or punishment of the former life. Each world and action, had an echo in eternity. Man's will acting fully and simultaneously through its vehicles, — the instinct, soul and intellect, — was capable of reaching the highest state of unification with God. This ideal of perfection, he taught could be achieved "by realization of truth in intelligence, of virtue in soul and purity in body." What a grand conception; what a beautiful picture? Who would not like to follow this ideal, so beautifully outlined by one of the greatest of Grecian seers, who himself led the life of perfection and experienced in his own self the deep truths and mysteries of God, like the prophets of various religions, and which he afterwards elaborated with such precision and care.

11

Tibetan Mystics

Tibet is the land of meditation houses. It is the home of the mystics. In no part of the world has Buddhism in its purest essence flourished so well as in the land of the *lamas* and mystic saints. Its natural scenery, its unique geographical grandeur, its enchanting solitude and its seclusion from the blur and blaze of modern civilization, have made Tibet an ideal land for the highest religious practices. In this country of snow and bitter cold, surrounded by mountains and deep ravines, there is so much of serenity and silence, that every one is a mystic or wants to become a mystic. Mysticism prevades as if it were through out the entire strata of Tibetan population.

Tibetan monks do not necessarily live in communities; each one is allowed to live in his own house or in any part of it. A life of austerity is enjoined upon them. If a monk be without any means of livelihood, he is allowed to earn his living by employing his time in some useful and beneficent profession, such as that of a teacher or a preacher. Just as in India, in Tibet also each disciple is allowed to take a guru, who is looked upon as his spiritual lord and whose injunctions, the disciple has to faithfully carry out.

The religious world of Tibet is divided into two sections. One part consists of those who advocate and adhere strictly to the Eightfold Path chalked out by the great Buddha, as the means of attaining nirvana. The other section consists of the intellectuals who do not submit themselves to any obligations or prescribed laws. They choose what is called the "Short Path" or the "Divine Path" to achieve *nirvana.* Such a short path is recognised as dangerous by the advanced monks, who rightly insist upon the necessity of a *chela* going through the entire purification process before he hazards to seek God by means of meditation and contemplation. The virtues, the practice of which should form the background of each disciple's initiation in the path of salvation, are abstinence and chastity, detachment, righteousness, compassion, gentility, charity, kindliness of thought, word and action, utter selflessness, absolute quietness and control of the mind.

In Tibet, meditation is a most common feature in the life of a Tibetan, be he a monk or a layman. Even an ignorant peasant is told to meditate. Some meditate and succeed in securing some powers, which they display to eke out an indolent living.

Miss Alexander David Neil is a talented author of several works on Tibetan Mystics, herself having lived in that land of adventure for many years. She relates some stories, which give an idea of the miraculous effects of meditation. She says, a rustic came to a lama and asked him to teach him meditation. And the monk, realising the mental aptitude of the enthusiast told him to sit in a quiet place and meditate on a yak. This simpleton did as he was directed and after some time when the monk came back to him to find out his progress, asked him to come out from the secluded apartment. The rustic said,

"How can I come out, the door is too small. These horns of mine do not allow me to get out." By meditating on "yak" the simpleton had magnetized himself in the thought that he had become a yak with horns.

A nun came to a monk, who was fat and sturdy and asked for a meditation prescription. The monk jocularly told him, "Meditate on me. Think that you are carrying me on your shoulders." The nun practised as she was told but after some time, she felt the load so heavy and painful, that she substituted the monk for herself and imagined that she was carried by the monk and not that she was carrying him. The result was the feeling of heavy load disappeared.

A Tibetan was told to meditate on his *guru* as sitting on his head. As he was walking, he stumbled and he got so frightened, that the guru sitting on his head had fallen in the valley that he made a desperate search for him in that place.

Such is the creative power of concentration and meditation. It is no wonder, if those who practise meditation become magicians, whether good or bad, according to their temperaments and motives. We have referred to White Magic and Black Magic in our Chapter on Magic in the foregoing pages. In Tibet also there are two classes of magicians. There are those who are not able to gain complete mastery over the secrets of nature but are able to get in communion with certain entities, whom they invoke by means of *mantras*, charms and various other devices. They coerce these supra-physical elements to carry out their orders. They are known as sorcerers.

But the true type of magician is the mystic who meditates purely for the purpose of obtaining *nirvana*, liberation of his own soul, and does not care for supernormal powers. These powers come to him naturally but but does not make use of them, for the goal of his life is pure salvation. He knows also that he himself is the origin of supernormal powers, unlike the sorcerer, who is dependent upon the outside agencies, to carry out his will. These adepts are the highly evolved souls, who seek compete seclusion in contrast with the other class made up of sorcerers, soothsayers, necromancers and occultists, who make a display of their powers out of self-gratification.

Development of psychic forces is most commonly resorted to by the Tibetans. The higher and better class of religious monks do not approve of such practices, as it is fundamentally irreligious and not in conformity with Buddha's teaching, the object of which is pure salvation and nothing else. We know the answer which Buddha gave, when he came across an emaciated Indian yogi, who had made *tapas* and practised meditation for twenty five long years and had eventually gained the power of walking on the waters of the river. "My poor fellow, have you really wasted so much years for such a trifling result? Why, the ferry man will take you to the opposite bank for small coin."

Madame Alexandra David Neil devotes a whole chapter in her book. "*With Mystics and Magicians in Tibet*" on Psychic Sports, indulged in by Tibetan monks. She gives descriptions of the feats of a *lung-gom-pa*. The latter as a result of long practice can walk miles and miles away, with out a stop, for more than 24 hours at a stretch. When he walks, his feet hardly touch the ground. He may stumble over a sharp edged stones, or thorny bushes, but a strange kind of anaethesia so deadens the sensations, that he does not feel hurt in any way. He does not walk; he glides swiftly as if on a snow covered lake. Nay, he flies, his feet hardly touch the ground.

In India, nakedness is symbolical of utter renunciation. In Tibet, those who practise meditation for the purpose of acquiring occult powers, indulge in nakedness, as a measure of their power of endurance. In cold, bleak nights, even when storms thunder and rains pour with a heavy thud, when water freezes and icy cold wing blows one to pieces, it is not uncommon to come across mystics in Tibet, who would meditate uncovered in body, in the freezing weather, on bare ground, without any covering or shelter on the summit of a Tibetan mountain or in the midst of the deep gorge of a valley. This power of endurance in a Tibetan hermit is due to his developing by means of meditation a certain kind of fire in his body, which protects him from external cold, just as we protect our body by warm clothes. This secret fire called in Tibetan language *tumo.* It is not ordinary heat. It is the possession of an inner sensation of force mystically produced when the mystics go into ecstasies or raptures. To speak in the words of Madame Alexandra David Neil, "In the secret teaching *tumo* is also the subtle fire which warms the generative fluid and drives the emergy in it, till it runs all over the body along the channels of veins, arteries and nerves."

What are the qualifications for *tumo* practices? The candidate must be skilled in various practices connected with breathing so very common with our Indian yogis. He must be skilled also in perfect concentration of the mind and must be capable of going into trance. He must possess a strong constitution. When he does the breathing exercises he must breathe out hatred, anger, lust, cupidity, sloth, and stupidity. And when he breathes in, he must invoke the blessings of the great Buddha, who made the great renunciation and other saints and sages.

The aspirant has to control his mind and having attained perfect calmness, he imagines a golden lotus on the level of the navel. In this lotus, there stands like a shining star, the syllable *ram.* Above the syllable *ram* is the syllable *ma* and it is said by meditating on the navel and imagining the syllables of ram and ma, a feminine deity issues called *Dorji Naljorma.* By meditating in this manner and identifying himself with the deity which emerges, the aspirant acquires ecstasic heat or fire.

Telepathy is also practised in Tibet Just as we hear London, Moscow, Paris, Berlin on the wireless. Tibetan monks mostly adepts can send their thoughts but without the medium of any physical instruments. It is a wireless telegraphy the subtler way of sending messages "on the wind." This power is achieved when the aspirant succeeds in completely quietening the mind from all cogitations and agitations and gaining complete oblivion of all things.

We have already said that the "Divine Path" or the "Short Cut" is hazardous but many monks and even laymen tread the path, with a view to reduce the number of years of probation to become fit for God realization. The path is dangerous from this point of view that if the aspirant is not able to fulfil the conditions of the path, he slides down spiritually and the short way eventually proves the longest way in realizing his heart's desire. The aspirant must first get instructions from an adept or an advanced anchorite of the monastry, to guide him on the path. The preliminary step in the path is living in seclusion. To "stay in *tsams*" means to live in isolation or seclusion.

There are meditation houses of various types. In Petanjali's *Sutras*, the different kinds of practice are classified in three groups viz. *dhyana, dharna* and *samadhi.* But in Tibetan Mysticism eleven kinds of consciousness are described each with a slight sleek of difference, exceedingly difficult to describe in our English phraseology. The meditation houses are of different types marked out for different classes of people. They are dark houses, isolated from civilisation. Some are partially and some are wholly dark. In some, the light of the sun is allowed to come and the sky is seen from the interior of the dark cell, but in others complete darkness prevails and no sun, no moon, no man, no woman are allowed to enter. These latter cells are like closed sepulchres. The aspirants that are locked up in such dark cells do not hear the voice of a visitor, not get the light of the sun even for an hour. Each one is left to himself to commune with and to unfold his latent powers by his own individual efforts. Each meditative hermit has an attendant. He brings him meals and leaves the food tray outside the door. If he fails to bring the daily food on account of any mishap or sickness, the meditative monk must not resent it or make a complaint. He must go without food.

Such a rabid type of imprisonment in a dark cell should be enough to send any man into a frenzy. We know of persons working in lonely light houses and those stranded by ship wreck, living in solitary isles. They go stark mad and lose their mental control. It is a terrible trial. But with the silent meditative monks, bent upon securing the secrets of nature and their salvation, it is not so. Meditation is their ally. It creates a joy in their hearts, which fills the void in the atmosphere. Strange lights and visions come to them while in a state of trance and the monotony and darkness of the cell are not felt.

The monks stay in these cells of darkness, sometimes for a few months, and sometimes for a few years. It all depends upon the ability and adaptibility of the aspirant and according to the instructions of the master.

When a mystic's term in a dark cell is about to come to an end, a small hole is made in one of the walls. This hole is daily made larger and larger, allowing the stream of sunlight in the cell to increase in graded volume. The idea is to make the hermit in the dark cell get re-accustomed to sunlight by graded steps, else it might do him harm, if he were delivered all of a sudden in the full blaze of the sun.

While meditating, the hermit repeats the mantra *'Aum mani padma hum'*, several times. This mantra is very significant. *Aum* is a Sanskrit word, most widely used by the Hindus in their devotion to Brahman at the time of meditation. It signifies God, the inexpressible Absolute, the One without a second, as pictured in the *Advaita* philosophy. According to Sri Shankacharya "*Aum*" is the chief support of meditation. In one of the Upanishads, it is compared to the bow by means of which the individual self attains universal Self.

Mani padma are also Sanskrit terms, meaning "the jewel of the lotus". The "jewel of the lotus" is Buddha's teaching. *Hum*, which is the end of the whole mantra is a war cry. It is a cry against "I", egotism. The significance of the whole mantra is that by introspective meditation, one must find "the jewel of knowledge, truth, reality, liberation, nirvana — these different terms being different denominations of one and the same thing."

The six stages of the mystic path are as under:

(1) The mystic must read books on religion and listen to learned discourses on religion and theology.

(2) He may choose any line of religion or teaching that appeals to him, by means of which he may be able to build up the foundation of his salvation.

(3) He must be humble and his mind must always rise above the sordid things of life. He should dwell in lofty thoughts and not make any show of his religiousness.

(4) He should be indifferent to praise or censure. He must have no attachment of any kind.

(5) He must look at the world quite unconcerned in any way.

(6) The sixth stage is the realization of the void.

This "void" is not annihilation that is so wrongly understood by the ignorant. There is no atheism in Buddhism. When a man becomes an *Arhat*; All his desires for evil completely vanishes. He becomes absolutely pure, sinless and he inevitably becomes fit for *nirvana*, which means ceasation from the wheel of birth and death. Madame Elavatsky says in "*Isis unveiled*", "*Nirvana* is the world of cause in which all deceptive effects or delusions of our senses disappear. *Nirvana* is the highest attainable sphere. To reach *nirvana* means absorption into the great universal soul. It means "intimate union" with the Highest and not annihilation. It is annihilation of matter and the triumph of the spirit.

When a man begins to realize that all phenomena are illusory that they emanate from the mind and they must sink in the mind, he realizes the goal of life — *nirvana*.

Meditation is given prime importance in mysticism, for the mystics realize that reason is a very poor substitute and a weak instrument in understanding the laws that are supernatural, the knowledge of which is hidden in the inner recesses of the soul itself. Buddhism excludes the conception of a personal God. But as we have said it is stupidity to identify Buddha's conception of *nirvana* with atheism. In fact, the sole aim and object of the Tibetan mystic is to find the deliverance of the spirit from the prison house of the physical body.

Tibetan mystics may be compared to the highest type of spiritual adventurers and sportsmen. They boldly plunge into fire, determined in their will, to pursue the quest of their heart to the very door of a living death, if need be. They have no fear for any consequences. They are the boldest and most adventurous types of mystics, unequalled by any except the Catholic mystics of the Middle Ages.

One of the vows which a Tibetan mystic takes on the Path of Beatitude is, "I will cause no suffering to any one." A story is related of a poor Tibetan Monk, who was given some coins by a traveller who accosted him. This monk had a disciple whose greed was aroused by the sight of the money. He mortally wounded his *guru* for the sake of filthy lucre and he cleared off in the jungle with the money. The monk was in terrible agony. But inspite of his terrible suffering he did not shout for help. He mitigated his pain by going into meditation. At last when the people from surrounding village came to him they found him lying in a pool of blood, suffering very acutely. They asked him why he had not shouted for help. His reply was, "If I had shouted for help you would have come immediately and would have pursued the man, who had run away with the money after stabbing me. I purposely refrained from crying for help, in order to give him a chance to escape. Now that he is beyond your clutches, I can die happily in the thought that I have not created any karma by becoming the cause of his affliction." And the monk breathed his last.

A story is related of a mystic who gave up his life to a hungry tigress. It is said that he went to a forest and saw a hungry tigress which had given birth to cubs, but she was so emaciated and weak that she had not the strength even to move an inch. This man quietly went near the tigress and offered himself as food. The ravenously hungry animal tore him to pieces and made a good meal of him.

The question is whether such a sacrifice is praiseworthy. Our reply is definitely in the negative. God does not want such sacrifices at all. The ultimate idea of a sacrifice is the real good of some cause or an individual. Let us reflect upon the sacrifice of Father Damien as a contrast. He was born in a Belgian home of Catholic parents devoted to God. The boy from his very young age showed a tendency for a religious and holy life. He would often play of a truant and escape from the school and his home to loiter in secluded places and pray and meditate. His young heart was full of God and God alone.

When he grew up, he became a priest and he was sent as a minister attached to a church in the far off Hawaii Islands. He took immense interest in his work but his interest soon ebbed, when he saw lepers abounding the church, uncared for. All that was done by the Government was to round up periodically all the street lepers and pack them off to a distant island to die without any attendance or care. It was a cruel way to dealing with the leper problem of the place.

Once when a ship was being loaded with lepers, along with their coffins—each leper was supposed to take his own coffin with him,—Father Damien, who was watching could not resist the urge to go along with the ill-fated passengers of the ship. Without intimating any one, he jumped into the fully loaded vessel and sailed away with them.

When the ship arrived at its destination in some wilderness he got down along with the lepers. It was a most strenuous work that he had undertaken. He started building log houses and eventually succeeded with the help and co-operation of Philippine Government to lay out and build a model leper colony in that far-flung distant island for the comfort of the unfortunate sufferers. He spent his whole remaining life with them. He lived with them, he fed them with his own hands, he nursed them and ultimately he died a leper.

Father Damien's was a true and noble type of human sacrifice. By his great sacrifice, the cause of the leper gained the ear of the world. Associations were started for the amelioration of the lot of these unfortunate sufferers and Damien's name to-day is a household word in every European town.

12

Jewish Mysticism

"Open thou mine eyes, that I may hold wondrous things out of Thy Law!

"My son, if thine heart be wise, my heart shall rejoice, even mine:

"Yea, my veins shall rejoice, when lips speak right things.

"Behold! The day of the Lord cometh and it shall come to pass in that day,

"That the light shall not be clear nor dark, but it shall be one day,

"And the Lord shall be King over all the earth: in that day shall be

"ONE JEHOVAH

"And His Name shall be

"ONE"

The Chaldean teachings of the arcanean science were handed over from by one generation to another by the word of the mouth but later on, these teachings were put to writing, a copious use being made of symbols and allegories to hide the inner meaning Cabala is a term used for the mystical writings and interpretation of the Jewish Scriptures by the rabbis. It treats of the nature of

God and the universe. Jewish religion is essentially monotheistic. When the Jewish religion began to decline and it was exhausted, the mystical side of its Scriptures was revealed. The rabbis discovered that the whole creation of God, including man, the crown of His creation was a process of emanation from God; that God was immanent and every being, whether animate or inanimate, had a spark of divinity. The Cabalists assume that every letter, word, number and even accent of the Scriptures has an inner meaning. It is not our purpose, nor have we any knowledge to deal with the subject in any detail.

Madness is somehing divine. Moses dreamt of a Promised Land. He made his followers to go through a heavy travail. For full forty years, he drove them through a desert of doubt. They rebelled; they killed; they suffered; they died of hunger and starvation. But such was the divine faith in Moses, that after a long struggle he was able to win the hearts of his people, and he established the religion of Jehovah — One God, One Law, One Life. What he had learnt from the Egyptian hierophants regarding Isis and Osiris, he now revealed to his people, having himself realized the secrets of nature.

The secrets of the Cabala were given only to the initiates i.e. to those selected disciples whose earnestness and purity made them eligible for the sacred teaching. But Chassidism, founded by the Rabbi Israel ben Eliezar. Baalshem, — in the eighteenth century was taught to the unlettered also among whom he moved. Baalshem started life as a beadle in a small village church. He got God's vision and he imparted his secrets to his wife, both of whom then wandered from place to place, revivifying the teachings of yore and bringing the life of the ancient wisdom religion to the hearths and homes of the peasants and other common folk. They had long subjected themselves to the oppression and tyranny of the Rabbis, whose learning appeared to them as uncouth and unintelligible. Baashem gave the teaching of a joyous religion. It was not a jargon of formalities, conventions, superstitions, creeds and dogmas. It did not include metaphysical disputations.

He taught the people that deliverance lay in simple-minded devotion to God and in sanctity of life and not in learning and deep thinking. What was wanted was not the knowledge of the intricacies of the Law but the teaching of pure heart, a pure mind, that could be engrossed in divinity. He discarded the outward formalities and inculcated into the hearts of the people the longing and love for God, who was pictured as the Alone, the Supreme, who created the universe, out of void and sent into that creation. His own glory or presence — the *Shechina*. Every particle of the universe was a part and parcel of the Divine Being. The sparks from God fell upon all beings, whether animate or inanimate and these "imprisoned sparks" must eventually return back to the primordial source of existence. This return journey of the human soul, he showed was in following the path of sanctity, in creating a state of holiness within oneself. Ecstasic joys, ecstasic sings were the outward manifestations of the inner sense of holiness and purity. The redemption of the world lay he taught not by the method of mortification of the flesh nor in the comprehension of the subtleties of thought. Metaphysics and mortification were taboo to him. Just as night broadens into daylight, the evil in man, the darkness in him must give place to the light of righteousness and goodness for only by sanctity of heart and mind could God be realized.

There are two words commonly used in Chassidism — *Hitlahabut* and *Karana*. *Hitlahabut* means a rapturous longing for absorption into the Godhead. It is a key to Immortality, Eternity. If a man were to fulfil all the commandments and be even possessed of wisdom but if he did not feel any fervour or joy for the Divine in earthly life, he would not feel the impulse of divine joy in his heavenly life. It is a long way to reach this stage of divine ecstasy. It has to be attained by slow steps. The soul cannot get itself absorbed into the Eternity, at one jump. It is a slow process.

In the Vedas this final stage is called *samadhi*, the entire absorption of self into the Over-Self. *Hitlahabut* is the ecstasy of the divine beyond time and space. It is the "mystic meal". When man dismisses from his mind everything that is earthly, he enters into this final stage of absorption into the Divine.

By *Karana* is meant not only the aim or intention but the goal. It is the goal of redemption. "It is redemption that the Shechina should return from exile, that all the husks should fall off from the "Splendour of God', which should purify itself and become free and unite with its Lord in complete unity." (*Jewish Mysticism* by Professor Martin Buber, Translated from the German by Lues Cohen).

Chassidism, like all other mystic teachings, embraces the belief in the cycle of births and re-births, for in one life of flesh, it is so difficult for a soul to redeem itself and be united with the Absolute Spirit. The Chassidic makes use of his will to convert the external into the internal. The divine joy lies in the heart and when all things are reduced to the inward feeling of naught, when the mind ceases to be attached to anything that is earthly, it becomes prepared for entering into the final stage of absorption into God. Holy communion, holy enjoyment —

these are the pincers by which can be seized the nut of God-realization.

Very great stress is put in Chassidism on the teaching of love. Buddha said, "Hatred ceaseth not by hatred; hatred ceaseth by love." And Zaddi Rabbi Raphael said,"If a man sees that his companion hates him, he should love all the more. For the communion of the living is the chariot of the "Splendour of God" and if there is a rift in the chariot, it must be filled up and where there is so little love, that the joint falls apart man must increase the love on his side in order to supply the want." The Christ's teaching. "Love thy neighbour as thy self" is a lever towards the accomplishment of true renunciation.

"Love is the omnipotence of the ideal. To love is to live, to love is to know, to love is to be able, to love is to pray, to love is to be the Man-God." When the world understands and realizes the depth and force of love, its spiritual fibre and its immortal vision, it will be redeemed of all its sorrows and sins. Love is forgetfulness of self; it is suppression of ego; it is extinction of desire; it is symbolism of unity with all, — union with God.

13

Sufism

Islam is purely a monotheistic religion. Mohomed is deemed to be a prophet, who got his revelation through the angel Gabriel, but the teaching contained in the Holy *Koran* does not give indication of that inner vision of the true and entire secrets of the universe. It speaks no doubt of the sublimity and unity of God who created the universe and laid down the law of good and evil. Mohamed was chiefly a law giver, a reformer, a statesman, a warrior and the religion he preached was unique in this respect, that it was quite sufficient to meet the exigencies of the time in which he lived. It helped him in coalescing the warring elements and in reducing the immorality and corruption that were rampant among the Bedouins. The *Qoran* is considered by the followers of Islam as a book of revelation. We do not want to enter into any controversy on the subject.

Several centuries after Mohamed, Mohamedan mysticism came into existence. We mean Sufism. It was a reaction, chiefly of Persian mind, against the narrow conception of God, as an arbitrary agent, separate and apart from His creation. These sufis as they were called were none else than those Iranians, the followers of the religion of Zarthustra, who were compelled by the followers of Islam, when they conquered Persia to abandon their religion and to become Mohamedans. Some fled from Iran but a large majority were converted into Islam at the point of the sword. But the faith in their original religion continued to burn secretly in their heart. Zarthustra had taught their ancestors that God was both transcendental and immanent and that it was possible for a person to see God, to know God, and to become one with God. This grand conception of God secreted long before inwardly found expression at last in the form of Sufism. We emphatically state that Sufism of Iran was not a new fangled religion but a version of the old Iranian religion which flourished centuries ago. It was a reflection of the esoteric teachings of the long forgotten Zoroastrianism.

The Sufis revolted against the orthodox Mohamedanism, not only because they were against the dogmas, conventions and formalities of the Islamic Church, but more so, as the idea that God revealed Himself to Prophet Mohamed only and will not reveal Himself to anyone else was extraneous to their vision. They held that God dwelt in the heart of every person. The spark of God was latent in every being, whether human or not human and that every man could be a prophet. The paths lending to the union with God, which is the mystic's goal of life are as many as the breaths of the nostril.

Sufism was a sort of spiritual religion outside Islam, based on pantheism. To the Sufis God is not a mere abstract idea but an indwelling, all pervading, Absolute Spirit — the Universal Mind, — the sparks of which animate the whole nature.

Sufism is mysticism in this sense that it recognises the impermanence of earthly possessions and attractions and enjoins upon its followers to lead a life of purity and austerity. To the Sufis, God is One and Life is One. The heart is the "Palace of the Beloved." He yearns to meet his Beloved, but this longing of his can not be satisfied unless he loves all mankind equally without distinction of any kind.

The Sufi's mental attitude is liberal. He takes in his conception all and everyone, whether rich or poor, good or bad, virtuous or sinner. To him all are part and parcel of One Divinity, whom he loves, adores and worships with a fervour that knows no bound, no limit. The Sufi recognises no outside authority. He is not a slave to any conventions; he belongs to no institutional organisation. No temple, no *math*, no mosque, no school, no caravan is his centre. He is like a free bird tied to no cult or school. His own dwelling place is his *math* and mosque. He is free to roam about wherever he likes. His heart is his gospel. He takes pride in his poverty.

We may divide the Sufis into two categories. There is the mendicant Sufi that goes from door to door and begs his living. He has renounced life and has nothing to do with worldy affairs. In Arabia, this mendicant class are called fakirs. The word is derived from the Arabic phrase *Elfakir, fakhri* meaning "Poverty is my pride." In Persia, the word used is *Dervish*. It means the sill of the door. The word Sufi is derived from the word "*Suf*" meaning wool. The original Sufis used to put on a robe of coarse wool. The Sufis spread over Egypt, Turkey, Persia and Hindustan. The mendicant class lives by mendicancy and by pursuing the art of jugglery. Most of them form the scum of the society. They are not actuated by any sense of high idealism. They form a rabble of religious imposters, whose parasitic indolence deserves condemnation. But there is another class, the superior who do not make a display of their renunciation but lead a life of contemplation and quiet service.

If we turn to Persian literature, especially in the medieval ages, we come across such literary geniuses among the ranks of Sufis as have made a landmark in the history of the literature of the world. The *Shah Nama* by Firdosi is considered to be one of the greatest epics of the world. It gives an account of all the Persian Kings and their sovereignties. It is didactic as well as mystical. The fervour with which the poet describes the glories of the early Persian Shahs and the mystical trait of their characters, especially of Shah Kaikhushru, who after feeling disgusted with the world, evaporated, as it were, into thin air,—so sudden was his vanishment—is indicative of something more than what we can see on the surface. Was Firdoshi a Mohamedan or a descendant of the ancient Iranians, proselytised by brute force and compulsion when the Persian Empire was run over by Mohamedans in the reign of the last King Yezdogard III some twelve centuries ago?

Among the Sufi poets who have left immortal names may be mentioned Hafiz, Sheikh Saadi, Jalaluddin Rumi and Farid-uddin Attar 'of ancient Iran. They give an allegorical cover to clothe the Sufistic doctrine. They speak rapturously of the Beloved. The Beloved is none else than God. The tavern is the oratory. The wine is not the physical wine but that state of superconsciousness, which is aroused when a man's heart is enraptured by the sense of a bewildering beauty—a conception of the Divinity.

Sheikh Saadi lived to a very old age. He was 120 lunar years old when he died. But his "*Bostan*" and

"Gulistan" are immortal works in which the immortal bard sings in a rapturous strain of the eternal beauty of God.

The poetry of Hafiz also indicates religious mysticism. The western critics do not consider the poems of Hafiz, Sufistic, for he led a dissipated life, being fond of wine and women. When he died, there was a strong opposition against burying him in the sacred enclosure. It was then that in accordance with the custom of the time, the subject of controversy was left to divination. One of the books of Hafiz's poems was opened at random and the finger pointed at the following verse:

"Turn not thy feet away from the bier of Hafiz, for though immersed in sin, he will be admitted in Paradise."

The Mohamedan admirers of Hafiz read in his odes and verses a mystical fervour for God. There is one single idea running throughout all his verses. To one unaccustomed and not trained in Sufistic culture, the utterances of Hafiz appear sensuous and degrading. But Hafiz, though he led a life of dissipation, was a Sufi at heart and he employed the Sufistic technique in his poems as usually done by other Sufis. Hafiz really was not a Sufi in practice but, in spite of his weaknesses, he must have had genuine love for God, which he gave expression to in his cooler and sedate moods of thought. His poetry was spontaneous and natural. We see in his poems a longing and an yearning for the Beloved — a fervent cry of the soul to escape from the imprisonment of the body.

The other great pantheistic writers are Jalal-uddin Rumi and Farid-uddin Attar, both Sufis of a high order.

It is said of Farid-uddin Attar that he was a seller of drugs in the beginning but, later on, he took to versifying and he has left immortal works. He was a highly religious man and led a life of austerity, simplicity and purity. In fact, he had renounced life and was given to devotion and comtemplation of God. His poems and other works teem with mysticism of an exalted nature. The conception of the Sufis is in no way different from other mystics. They believed that God existed alone and he created the universe merely by His Will. He uttered the word "Be" and the whole universe became manifest. God being immanent in nature, every soul in man must eventually after various births return to its original home which is the abode of God. The soul of man is a spark that has emanated from the Splendour of God and it must eventually be absorbed in the fire of the Splendour of God.

Farid-uddin Attar has written many *masnavis* among which *Pandnama*, the *Book of Counsels* and *Mantik-Uttair*, the *Speeches of Birds* occupy a high place in Persian literature. The latter is an allegorical poem in which the Sufistic idea of the absorption of the Soul in the Deity is very beautifully portrayed "interspersed with moral tales and pious contemplation." The allegory runs as under:

There are seven valleys, through which the birds travel. These valleys are the seven stages or stations on the path of the Mystics. At the end of the seven stages or the seventh valley is the phoenix or Simurg. If the birds do not succumb on the way and reach the phoenix, they attain *Fana* i.e., *nirvana*, liberation from earthly rounds.

Jalal-uddin Rumi is another Sufi poet whose poetic compositions have earned him immortal fame. He speaks of "celestial love" in his immortal work, *Yusaf* and *Zulaikha*. God is allegorically represented as the Beloved. The poem is intended to reveal God's beauty; that, union with God can only be achieved by true divine love and through the channel of purification; that passion is the idol which has to be broken to pieces; that, true love is an emanation from the Light of God.

The following is a moving appeal for deliverance from the world of ignorance:

"O God deliver us from pre-occupation with wordly vanities and show us the nature of things as they really are. Remove from our eyes the veil of ignorance and show us things as they really are. Show not to us non-existence as existent nor cast the veil of non-existence over the beauty of existence. Make this phenomenal world the mirror to reflect the manifestations of Thy beauty and not a veil to separate and repel us from Thee. Cause these unreal phenomena of the universe to be for us the sources of knowledge and insight and not the cause of ignorance and blindness. Our alienation and severance from Thy beauty all proceed from ourselves. Deliver us from ourselves and accord to us knowledge of Thee"

(Selection from Jalal-uddin Rumi's *The Lawah.*)

In the following passage we get a fine description of "The Absolute Beauty."

"The Absolute Beauty is the Divine Majesty endued with (the attributes of) power and beauty. Every beauty and perfection manifested in the theatre of the various grades of beings is a ray of His perfect beauty reflected therein. It is from these rays that exalted souls have received their impress of beauty and their quality of perfection. Whosoever is wise derives his wisdom from Divine Wisdom."

In the following lines we get a beautiful picture of how the consciousness of One God Alone can be achieved by the aspiring Sufi:

"In like manner, as it behoves thee to maintain the said relation continuously, so it is of the first importance to develop one quality thereof by detaching thyself from mundane relations and by emancipating thyself from attention to contingent forms; and this is possible only through hard striving and earnest endeavour to expel vain thoughts and imaginations from thy mind. The more these thoughts are cast out and these suggestions checked, the stronger and closer this relation becomes. It is, then necessary to use every endeavour to force these thoughts to encamp outside the enclosure of thy breast and that the "Truth" the most glorious may cast His beams into thy heart and deliver thee from thyself and save thee from the trouble of entertaining His rivals in thy heart. Then there will abide with thee neither consciousness of thyself, nor even consciousness of such absence of consciousness — nay there will abide nothing save the ONE GOD ALONE."

The following beautiful poetic lines give an indication of the human urge for God, the Beloved:

"O Thou whose sacred precincts none may see,
Unseen, Thou makest all things seen to be;
Thou and we are not separate, yet still
Thou hast no need of us, but we of Thee.

None by endeavour can behold Thy face,
Or access gain without pre-eminent grace;
For every man some substitute is found,
Thou hast no peer, and none can take Thy place.

Of accident or substance Thou hast naught,
Without constraint of cause Thy grace is wrought

Thou can'st replace what's lost, but it Thou are lost

In vain a substitute for Thee is sought.

In me Thy beauty, love and longing wrought;
Did I not seek Thee, how wouldst Thou be sought?

My love is as a mirror in the which
Thy beauty into evidence is brought.

O Lord none but Thyself can fathom Thee,
Yet every mosque and church doth harbour Thee;

I know the seekers and what 'tis they seek.—
Seekers and sought are all comprised in Thee."

The last line "Seekers and sought are all comprised in Thee" is a most significant statement of the Mystic's awareness of God and Oneness of Life.

The "*Fana*" of the Sufi, is the same as "*Nirvana*" of the Buddhist and "*Samadhi*" of Vedantin. All of them — the Sufis, the Buddhists and the Vedantins alike speak of the unreality of the seeming world and their goal is the absorption of the soul in the ocean of the Reality, that is, God.

India is a land of mystics and *sadhus*, but it is painful to note that inspite of our advance in knowledge, revolting methods of self-torture are still practised by our Indian anchorities, in some places. Such practices do develop will power and will is the greatest factor in spiritual life. But these methods of self-destruction for the purpose of exalting the soul and purifying the body are too antediluvian. Persian Sufism is a happy escape from such fantastic methods of uplifting the soul. The mysticism of the Persian Sufis, is less intense, but it is "more practical, more airy and more literary in character." Sufism has inspired many Persian poets, who have left immortal works.

A celebrated doctor of Heart propounded fifteen questions on the subject of Sufism and *Gulshan-i-Raz* composed by Sa'duddin Mahmad Shabistan is an answer to that questionnaire. It is not our purpose to enter into any details.

There is similarity between Persian Sufism and mediaeval Catholic Mysticism. Both systems exalt the "inner light" and both decry outward ceremonies, forms, creeds and dogmas, which are man-made. Formalism and ritualism have no place in the makeup of a Sufi or a Catholic Mystic. Both indulge in a similar phraseology viz. "Union with God", "Love for God", "Death to self", "Life eternal", "The indwelling spirit in man", "Grace and spiritual illumination". Both exhibit the same yearning and passionate longing for God only with this difference that the Sufis call God, the Beloved, the European mystics hail Him as "Father."

Mysticism is a religion of the heart and when the heart is touched, it is natural that there should be divine ecstasies accompanied even by rapturous dancing and singing. Both Sufism and Catholic Mysticism speak of such exalted states of "visionary raptures and supernatural exultations." The external phenomena sink into nothingness and the dominance of the Universal Spirit is felt in every tree and budding flower, in every man and woman, in every tiny drop of water, in every crystal of the star. It is no wonder that the mystic rapt in the thought of the encircling Beloved, loses himself in reptures and ecstasies.

> "The worlds of command and of creatures proceed from one breath,
> And the moment they come forth they go away again.
> Albeit here there is no real coming and going,
> Going, when you consider it; is naught but coming.

Things revert to their proper original,
All are One, both visible and the invisible."

(*Gulshan-i raz Exordium*)

Sind has been a land of Sufis and it has produced some eminent Sindhi Sufi poets; like Latif, Sachal, Rohal, Sami, Badil, Bekus, Dalpat and Sadik. The Sufi's path consists of three steps The first one is the affirmation of the clothings and wrappings of the flesh. The physical senses have to be trained and the unreality of the phenomena of the senses has to be grasped. This must lead to a struggle and we come to the second stage namely, when the Sufi begins to negate. He has to suppress his emotions, he has to trample his individuality and crush it.

"So long as thou art concious of thy individuality
So long there is no prayer. Give up your individuality
and then say your prayer."

The third step is an indication of the triumphant march over all the inward struggles of emotions, passions, attachments, prejudices, likes and dislikes, hatred, jealousy, love for ostentation, love for name and fame and riches. It means complete renunciation and freedom from earthly attachments. It means liberation of the soul. It is a dissolution of affirmation and negation, a solemn avowal of the mystic marriage of the soul with the spirit.

Let us hear Sachal's song of ecstasy:
"What are we? O what are we?
Brethren we know what we are.
Now we rejoice and say, "We know ourselves"
Now we cry, "What are we? O what are we?
Now clouds pour showers cool
Now burn fires of hell,

Now my heart is full of peace
Now tears flow in streams.
O Sachal, thou art the very He,
Why should we illusions weave."

The following beautiful lines of Latif will be read with interest:

He Himself is the splendour of the Splendid
He Himself is the soul of beauty
He Himself is the form of the Beloved
He Himself is beauty complete,
He Himself is teacher
He Himself is pupil,
He is thought Himself,
All this is known within the soul.
He Himself gives the message,
He Himself is the King,

He Himself takes care of Himself,
He Himself knows Himself,
He Himself sees Himself,
He Himself loves Himself,
He Himself creates abundantly,
He Himself longs for His created,
He is this He is that,
He is the Lord of Death, He is the Lord of life,
He is foe, He is friend,
He is here, He is there,
He lives in the mind,
He Himself sees the Light Himself."

(*Shah Latif*)

The following lines illustrate the struggle of a Sufi to win the goal of union with God:

"Drink thou thine own blood,
There is no better wine than that;
Strike thy teeth into thine own heart
There is no better meat than that.
Enter into the abode of desirelessness and see Allah,
The road of the spirit is as clear as the day,
Only desires have hidden it."

(*Shah Latif*)

14

Spiritualism

As a man evolves, his consciousness increases and he is able to perceive more and more of the grandeur and loveliness of the universe. His conception of God, as the Ultimate Reality, the Dispenser of Law and Justice, becomes more firmly rooted in his mind — nay he strives to become attuned with the Universal Spirit. But there is a difference between an occultist and a spiritualist. The former develops the innate, latent powers in him, by means of study, hard work, selfishness and yoga practices of a high order. The spiritualist on the other hand develops his psychic powers, which are inherent in every man but which in some persons become patent very soon. Psychism is a gift, no doubt, but its danger is that it can easily be abused without proper moral and self restraining training.

There is an innate desire in man to know from whence he came, what is the object of life, what is his final destination. Religion throws light on these problems but the hard hearted materialist wants a proof of everything and he can not be satisfied with explanations that require a mere trust in the experiences of others. Religion based on mere faith has no appeal to a man dominated by reason and logic. It was therefore inspite of religious teachings, Europe for a number of years was dominated by a class of people called Rationalists, who doubted the existence of God and had no belief in the immortality of the soul. Modern spiritualism which is the growth of the last one hundred years has rendered a great service in shattering the false idol of the Western Materialism.

For many centuries in the past, Science and Religion were at loggerheads. Science which was rooted in matter refused to acknowledge the presence of spirit. Man turned away from religion from other points of view too. The teachings of the church were intermingled with so much of dogma, ritual, creed and formalism that the intellect revolted. But when Spiritualism cut asunder the veil and revealed the knowledge of the existence of the invisible words it brought Religion and Science erstwhile antagonists into mutual alliance. The following extract from the speech of the Archbishop of York, delivered some years ago, is of considerable interest:

"The middle of the 19th century was marked by constant collision between scientists and theologians. Science was uplifted by its marvellous successes in discovery and invention. It was full of the aggressiveness of self-confidence. Theology, unprepared for the new views of the world which were opened out, tended to behave as older men are wont to do in the presence of militant and self-confident youth—to be resentful and dogmatic. Surely, we are coming to the time when science and religion, across their separate spheres, now more fully recognised, are stretching out hands of need and desire for one another. The man of religion must see that his knowledge of God is meagre and one-sided when he knows something of the wonderful ways in which God expresses himself in the process of nature.

The man of science, pausing sometimes in his patient tracking of the laws of nature, must hear a voice saying — what or who is the basis of this marvellous and all pervading unity of law? Now, largely under the influence of science, we have come to a greater and grander conception of God."

The record of the Church in Europe was not clean. It had burned many a Bruno, had punished many a Kepler, it had persecuted many a Gallileo. The Inquisition in Europe presents a melodramatic record of blood baths of the innocent. The London Dialectic Society was formed in 1869, "for the purpose of investigating the phenomena alleged to be spiritual". This society was composed of eminent scientists, the foremost of whom was Sir William Crookes, who took personal interest in investigating the phenomena of spiritism and was thoroughly convinced, as were his colleagues. The society made a report in favour of Spiritualism. Though the findings of the Committee were repudiated by various journals in England, the foundation stone of the Temple of Spiritualism was surely laid.

Even to-day Spiritualism has many opponents, specially Theosophists who have reviled it in season and out of season. If the attacks of the Theosophists were directed upon the methods used and the meagre success achieved by the so called Spiritual circles and seances, we would not have have any hesitation in siding with them. But certainly it cannot be denied that Spiritualism is a Science of Truth. It is still in its infancy and there is a scope of its greater usefulness in the future.

We have dealt with various kinds of spiritual phenomena and various aspects of this Science of Truth, better called Spiritual Philosophy in our book, "*The Other World*" and we shall not reconsider the subject. The centre of the whole spiritual teaching is God, the Law, the Creator, the Benefactor.

Christ said, "In my Father's house, are many mansions". (John Chapter XIV–2). And the science of Spiritualism reveals these mansions as various planes, — the astral, the mental and spiritual, which the soul has to go through and sojourn for a time till it returns back to the physical body. As A.P. Sinnet says, "The Spiritual realm is the proper habitat of the soul". The Higher self, which is the "non-material stable portion of the soul" as beautifully described by Sinnet, permanently dwells in the spiritual plane. In every human being, the Higher self is dormant. The object of life is to arouse this higher self latent in man. When we sleep, our higher self visits the spiritual planes. But it forgets its experiences when it returns back to the physical body. It is only when the lower self, getting its impress from the higher self gains victory over the temptations of physical life, for which several incarnations are necessary, that the soul advances and it becomes conscious of its Higher Self.

It must be stated that the spiritual plane is not the heaven, the place of eternal rest in the presence of God, as described in the Scriptures. The occultists and spiritualists of the higher order, confirm that the spiritual plane is only a resting house to which the soul goes and stays there for a considerable length of time, say ten to twenty centuries, before it goes back to the physical plane and is reincarnated. No new *karma* is engendered. No fresh causes are set in motion. In the astral and mental planes, objective results are sought. In the spiritual plane there is full consciousness and no effort is required in realizing thought. The higher planes are formless. Thought is the language of the spirits. Instead of forms, there are vibrations. The whole universe hangs on vibrations.

When we communicate with the other world bridging the gulf of matter and spirit, it is the spirit incarnate in the physical body, that speaks with the spirit, which is without any body. The discarnates are the spirits on the invisible planes and the incarnates are persons on the terrestrial plane. The latter are also spirits but they are imprisoned in matter and therefore not free.

We should not be misunderstood. We advocate the cause of Spiritualism but it is Higher Spiritualism and not spiritualism of the seance room. The people of the earth are still not sufficiently advanced spiritually. Most of them, when they shuffle off the moral coil, are able to reach only the astral plane and they are sent back to the physical plane for purification and gaining further experiences of physical life, after a short span of say fifty to hundred years, or even less. These discarnate spirits being earth-bound are ever eager to communicate with incarnate spirits in earth. As we have explained in "*The Other World*" the danger of the seance room is from the lower astrals and the elementals which hover round at the edge of the ethereal world. They may cause obsession, which is the greatest danger, the medium is exposed to.

Swami Vivekananda knowing the difficulties and dangers of the seance room and the fate of the medium indulging in constant communications with the discarnate spirits, was therefore quite justified when he made the following scathing attack on Spiritualism;

"Spiritualism has nothing to do with the display of psychic powers, which when analysed, show that man who deals with them is a slave of desire and a most egotistical person. Spirituality involves the acquisition of that true power which is character. It is the vanquishing of passion and the rooting out of desire. All this chasing after psychic illusions, which means nothing in the solution of the great problems of our life, is a terrible waste of energy; the most intense form of selfishness and leads to degeneracy of mind. It is this nonsense which is demoralising our nation. What we now need is strong common sense, a public spirit and a philosophy and religion which will make us men."

Leadbeater runs down public seances for obvious reasons but he speaks favourably of private family circle seances, as they are conducive to the growth of that moral, spiritual atmosphere, so very necessary in building up one's character and in making a permanent and tangible impression on life's journey and its goal. He says, in his work, "*The Hidden Side of Things*." This is infinitely the most satisfactory side of spiritualism for through it thousands of families communicate day by day with friends and relations who have passed from the physical world and in this way not only learn a number of interesting facts but are kept constantly in touch with spiritual subjects and at a high level of thought, with regard to them. Most commonly the central figure at these private seances is some departed member of the family and the communications ordinarily are affectionate sermonettes of a devotional character, often somewhat rhapsodical.

Occasionally, however where a departed relation happens to be a man of original thought or of a scientific turn of mind, a great volume of definite information is gradually gathered together.

We have quoted extracts from Swami Vivekananda and Bishop Leadbeater, both opposite views on Spiritualism, with the view that the reader may judge for himself. Spiritualism is a science of Truth. It gives knowledge of the realism of the worlds beyond. It is a source of great happiness if pursued with pure motives and purity of heart. But this very science becomes an instrument of the ruination of the medium and the sitters if they are not actuated by the highest of motives, but are victims of curiosity and egotism.

Leadbeater denounces public seances and he is perfectly justified in doing so. We quote the following passage from his work, *The Hidden Side of Things*, for the purpose of clarifying the whole issue:

"Public seances to most outsiders represent the whole of Spiritualism. All sorts of people are admitted to these, usually on payment of a small sum of money and the entities who appear on the astral side are just as curious and conglomerate as those who attend on the physical. The highest astral types are not to be found among the habitues of such seances, as these, but there is usually a sprinkling of dead people who have devoted themselves to the idea of being useful to those still on the physical earth, by the exhibition of phenomena and by the giving of various small tests.

The aura of such a seance is usually on the whole somewhat unpleasant, for it attracts a great deal of attention in the astral world as well as in the physical and consequently, round everyone of them is always a clamorous crowd of the most undesirable entities, who are restrained only by force from pushing in and seizing upon the medium. Among the dangers, attending these seances is the possibility that one of these desperate creatures may seize upon any sensitive sitter and obsess him: worse still, that he may follow him home and seize upon his wife or daughter. There have been many such cases and usually it is almost impossible to get rid of any which has thus obsessed the body of a living human being."

"As the tree falls, so must it lie!
As the man lives, so must he die!"

Death is a gateway to the higher journey to the other worlds. It is a continuation of life in the higher spheres and the soul brings with itself the impressions of its occupations and aspirations of the last incarnation and though it has now shed its physical envelop, it continues its existence with the same thoughts that it had built up in the last life and progresses carrying its credit and debit account from plane to plane and enjoying and suffering according to the fruit of its actions on earth. The old Mosaic law ran; "And thine eye shalt not pity; but life shall go for life, eye for eye, tooth for tooth, hand for hand, foot for foot." According to Spiritualism, God is not an angry God relentless in avenging sin. Having created Law, it works according to the principle of justice laid down. But there is no such thing as eternal punishment. Spiritualism does not teach the eternal punishment of hell fire. It speaks on the contrary of the progress which the soul must make to reach the final goal of life through the stages of purification and suffering. Sir William E. Cooper describes Spiritualism in his book, *Where Two Worlds Meet*, as "a realization and cognisation of the science of Being, — as Being — an identification of immateriality of man and of his atonement with the eternal principle of that all permeating and of all immanent essence which we worship under the multinomous name of God. Being spiritual in its essential principles, it forms the connecting link or means of communication between the two worlds of Matter and

Spirit." (Page 188) This author goes so far as to state that Spiritualism preceded religion and it was its precursor. It was out of Spiritualism that sprang the old religions of the world, Zoroastrianism, Brahmanism, Buddhism, Confucianism, Taosism, Christianism, Mohammedanism and later on gave birth to Swedenborgianism and Theosophism. The temples of ancient Egypt, Greece, Chaldea, Iran, India, Assyria and Babylonia were built as if it were on the ground of Spiritualism. The ancients knew the intercourse between this world and the other world. Was not Christ a great medium? The miracles he performed were due to his yogic powers or to his intercourse with Divine Life which gave him the power of healing and resurrecting the dead from their graves. The following message from one of the beneficent spirits will be read with feeling of emotion and elevation:

"There is a bridge between earth and heaven over which the angles pass onwards to commune with the sons of men. That bridge builded of yore by God's merciful wisdom is reared upon the indestructible foundations of the Eternal and upon its mighty piers of rock divine had each spanning arc been built by angel and by man, out of the constructive elements of "Love" and "Service" each to the other given. God inspired, has this loving service been and God inspired and God endowed must Love for ever be. Continue then. Thou mighty Over Soul, this constructive work divine, so that to that wonderous Bridge of Love upreared, arch may grow from arch and pit from pier. Let that great viaduct be built so firm that man may pass over to angel and angel visit man — each to the other giving greeting sweet and holding loving commune.

"Thou everlasting, in whose mighty Unity blend the Motherhood and Fatherhood of God shower down on those workers on the earth plane — co-workers with us on this plane of life, whereon dwell we, Thy chosen instruments of communication with the sons of Men, that essence of Thy Love divine which flowing from out Thy bountiful Motherhood, may reach each living soul and light it through and through — as the steady radiance of Truth's lamp will in time illumine the dark places in each spirit being. May let this stream of all enveloping Love carry out on its broad beneficent bosom each spirit being on all Thy countless planes of life — so that every soul, floating on its boundless surface, may be borne onwards towards those portals of the Eternal, through which each spirit passing may find its promised Homeland."

The above spirit message reminds us of Jacob's ladder, where in the angels descended and men ascended and thus there was intercourse between the two worlds.

The psychic gift is an instrument of great value in the hands of the person, who has truly developed his spiritual qualities and is anxious to be utilised by the Higher Powers for evolutionary progress of all mankind, which is God's Plan and Design.

"And as I looked, lo! there appeared before my eyes all those scenes through which I had just passed and now I saw clearly and not through a darkened glass. And I said unto myself — Blessed Be The Light!"

The object of Spiritualism is to uplift the soul. Invariably, the man who receives a message from a high spirit feels a sensation of elevation. The atmosphere of sanctity and exaltation of spirit which pervades in a private seance, where members sit, tied in loving bonds, waiting for their dear departed ones, to teach them of God and the beauty of the wonder land where they live, can not but have a lasting effect upon their soul. It is of a far greater educative value than a sermon preached from a church pulpit. It has a ring of sincerity and solemnity and emits a spring of exultation. It brings down heaven to earth and raises the earth to heaven.

"And I feel a power uprising
Like the power of an embryo God;
With a glorious wall it surrounds me,
And lifts me up from the sod."

Henry Metcalf in his work, *The Evolution of Spiritualism* speaks rapturously of Spiritualism, which he describes as "scientific religion". The following extract from the above book gives us a gist of his eulogy:

"Spiritualism forms a true basis of philosophy to many thousands. For this reason alone it commands our respect; its missionaries have been divinely inspired to shape a true philosophy of life planting flowers of love and hope in unhappy bosoms no longer can it be considered on trial, but it is truly a moral giant stalking through the land to bring an understanding of infinite ideals and soul realization to the unfortunates of the human family. . . . If man were to sift the evidence of Spiritualism, he will at length perceive the coming of "heaven into the market place" and a development of his psychic consciousness producing a mental realization of the ineffable grandeur of life itself. Spiritualism will become a greater thing when it becomes generally known that the phenomena reveal a force — intelligence, and it is science according to the grammar of sciences."

There can be no doubt that the Spiritualist movement in Europe which has been gaining strength from year to year — it has produced a literature so extensive and voluminous that it completely overshadows the production of works on arts, history, economy, biography, politics, theology, and poetry, all put together, — has done immense good in bringing men and women nearer to God by shaking their materialistic outlook and cleansing their hearts of the gross of self-interest. It has purged religion of its fantasies and made men look upon it as the surest road to safety in the journey of life.

Of all the spiritual phenomena, spiritual healing should be put upon the highest pedestal. It is here that we get the most beneficent demonstration of the science. The cures effected by spiritual healing are not myth. The late pastor Rev. W. T. Parish of London of revered memory, who died only recently, was considered as the greatest spiritual healer of the world. He was a saintly man, extremely humble, loving, kind and compassionate to all. He worked strenuously, treating cases by thousands from afar and near, and all in the name of God, the most beneficent and just.

Silver Birch is one of the most favourite controls, who appears at most of seances held in England. His mission is to teach humanity simple homely truths, to help them to escape the horrors and desolateness of the journey after death, if left in ignorance. He sows the seeds of wisdom, as he bursts forth in eloquent language through the mouth of a medium.

"How do you see a new world being born ?" is the question asked and he replies:

"I see a plan, a divine plan. I see that the power of the spirit is the greatest power of the universe. Man may thwart and delay, man may impede and stay, but man can not for ever prevent the power of the spirit being made manifest. When you have the knowledge of spiritual truth, you have the key which unlocks all the doors of mankind's problems. I am not being unkind to all the sincere reformers, who moved by anger, by righteous wrath, or by an overwhelming sympathy for the down-trodden and the weak, feel to suppress wrong, to fight injustices, to enable all the bounties of the Great Spirit to be fairly distributed. They see only one part of a problem. They see physical needs that may be satisfied — perhaps they see mental needs that must be satisfied too — but pre-eminently man is a spirit, part of the Great Spirit, part of the power which fashioned all life. Man is not so infinitesimal that he is forgotten amidst the vast spaces of the universe. He is always part of the Great Spirit, contributing to the spiritual nature of the Infinite.

You can not stifle the power of the spirit; it must merge. It will triumph over cruelty and hatred, it will triumph over bludgeons, concentration camps, dictators, because the spirit of man must be as free as the air he breathes. That is his natural, divine, spiritual heritage. All those who have seen the vision splendid and have beheld the new world that is to be, know that it must be, because it is part of that same purpose which breathed into man and raised him from animal to human and will raise him again from human to divine. Your task is always to hand on the torch, rekindle its flame, so that the generation that comes after you will have greater light to illumine its pathway. The foundations have been laid. They were laid many years ago in our world. And gradually, painfully, laboriously, men and women of all denominations and of none, were raised up to be the witnesses of the eternal spirit to labour for the quickening of the divine plan. The new world must come."

Silver Birch in the course of his message, to the Spiritual Healing Centre, Coimbatore (India), said, "Remember that our (spiritual) plane is full of living beings who take great interest in the events of your world and occasionally we are awaiting reports of events and occurrences in your world. The present times look bad, but it is merely a prelude to the millenium that is to be. Ram Ram will be the prophet of the New Era. The great Master is building up the ideas for reforming the physical world and humanity. We are all cooperating with Him in His great work. His great ideas will go round the world and will be the foundation stone of the future. (Message delivered on 25-5-46)

The following is the text of the message of the great Master Rishi Ram Ram, rightly called the "Prophet of the New Era", that was delivered to the Centre on 25th December 1946:

"Humanity is entering upon a new era of constructive co-operation. Individuals have to keep the goal before them and co-operate with one another and with society as a whole. The world of humanity will become one family of nations when Peace and Amity will reign over them inspite of different colours, creeds or religions. The message for the New Era is "LOVE ALL . . . LOVE GOD and seek out more ways of loving Men and God.

The Divine Plan is being brought home to your Leaders. They will see the vision of unity, behind the surging humanity and life in all forms. Violence and non-violence are merely aspects of *Karma*. The complete *Karma* is the mental attitude behind the *Karma*. Violence born of love or a loving attitude as when your doctors used to cure, is only apparent violence. Violence born of an attitude of hatred is real violence. A son or servant refusing to discharge his duties in nonviolent in appearance but his *karma* born of hatred is violence. Hatred is *Rajasic* energy and increases multiplied when hatred is returned for hatred. Love is born of *Satvic* nature and quenches the fire of hatred, when it is returned for hatred. If you see the astral and mental counterparts, you will realise immediately how love is like oil on troubled waters and quenches the agitated mind and feelings. Hence love and fearlessness are the antidote and corrective to hatred and revengeful ire. So convert your enemy into friend by love. Love will express itself between men as friendship and in society as cohesion binding it to-gether. Law, politics and various codes will hereafter be based on the binding force of love. Nations will form international friendships with other nations and make the sense of cooperation and amity, the future plank for ambassadors and political leaders. So no more of warring elements in the future world, no more use of weapons of destruction like the atom bomb. Go ye forth and speak of good will to all mankind and of love, love of God, love of all living creatures and love of the beings of the Higher Spiritual world who will be constantly watching you and guiding you. Om Santi Santi!"

The following is another message that was delivered by the great Master at the Spiritual Healing Centre on the same subject of the New Era, which will be read with particular interest, as it has a great bearing on the trend of the present day events.

"A New Era is opening out for mankind, a new era of World Religion, a new era of World Polity and a new Era of Knowledge and Wisdom. The world Religion will be broad-based like the great pyramids on Universal Love. The future humanity will climb towards Godhood through common prayers which will pull humanity heavenward. World Polity will be broadbased on Equality, Brother hood. Co-operation and Service which will support the great future edifice at the basicfoundation.

The new era of Science will open out to the scientists who will begin the study of the Inner Worlds of creation. Remember that Eternal Verities alone count. The evolution towards spiritual condition is the movement governed by the Immutable Law and every one of you should take your place in the movement which is the fulfilment of the destiny of all beings from the inanimate kingdom to the highest angels.

Cohesion is love and love binds mortals and immortals alike. Soul affinities survive death in the physical and astral planes. OM."

One of the most beautiful lessons that we learn from spirit messages is that we must attune ourselves to receive, "all inspiration, all wisdom, all truth, all knowledge" from the Higher Intelligenceies, for we ourselves are not original creators. We have only to be the receiving and transmitting stations. We have to become instruments in the hand of the Higher Ones who wield all power and energy to shape the worlds according to God's design. As we have free will the necessity of exercising that free will and to work in co-operation with the Higher Intelligences, who alone have the originating and creative power is so essential. The poet's song or the musician's compositions is not the result of his own creation or achievement. The capacity to be inspired by the Higher Ones is the case of the achievement.

"The difficulty is to achieve the process of attunement. If the laws that regulate conditions between the two states of life were perfectly understood, if the people of your world were to rid themselves of the many prejudices and superstitions which create barriers to a full and free communication, this wisdom of the Infinite could be poured through human instruments into your world. It always depends upon having an instrument to receive what we give and the ability of these instruments to attune themselves to receive the highest that can be given" (*Wisdom of Silver Birch*, page 85)

Is it not said in the Bible: "For its not ye that speak, but the Spirit of your Father which speaketh in you. (St. Matthew Chapter X–20)

Prayer is the mode of attuning ourselves to the higher realms. The whole purport of spiritual knowledge is that life continues. It is a part of "the great, eternal, creative life force." God the great White Spirit is the creator and regenerator. It is His power that sustains the universe. It is He who gives life and form to everything. His Law is Supreme, Unchangeable, Eternal, Inexorable. His Spirit girdles the whole world. Every one is born with the divine spark in him and each of us can become a recepticle for the divine wisdom to be poured into us for the perfection of this world, which is the goal of life.

15

Mysticism in Theosophy

CONTRIBUTION OF THEOSOPHY

In the olden years, when religious bigotry and intolerance were rampant and there was a feeling in man that the sacred knowledge of God should be imparted only to the few, who can understand and realize its sacredness and keep it in their hearts cherishing it as a great treasure, it was the universal practice in all ancient systems, to keep the doors of the secret teaching closed to all profane. The language which the occultists used for the propagation of their esoteric teachings was full of symbols and mystic signs. Allegories and fables played an important role in such occult teachings. Hierography, alchemic symbols, astronomical numbers and such other devices were resorted to by the occultists to keep the secret and sacred knowledge outside the purview of the profane.

The Theosophists have rent the veil and they have made a great contribution by broadcasting the secret knowledge through out the world.

Theosophy is wisdom-religion. It does not depend upon the scriptural stories of revelation but it applies the force of intellect as well as inner perception for the solution of all problems of life and of all phenomena, physical, psychical and spiritual. Down to the smallest atom, it knows that everything is a soul and that it moves and acts and has its being under the Law of Evolution, which is inherent in the whole.

Theosophy is a blend of religion and science. It is both a religious science and scientific religion. It ignores no factors. It deals with the whole in all its constituent parts. Its function is to explore into the regions of the inner faculties of man and to investigate into the phenomena of nature for the purpose of extracting the secrets of the universe.

Madame Blavatsky one of the founders of the Theosophical Movement may be considered as one of the greatest mystics of the modern age. Mysticism is the greatest of Eastern Wisdom. Deep love of God and utter renunciation of life in devotion to that Godhead which is the summit and essence of true Realization, are mainly Eastern teachings. It is no exaggeration to say that eastern wisdom in its transcendentalism far surpasses the western thought and culture. It is therefore surprising that the modern Theosophical Movement which is world-wide has sprung from western minds and that its principal pillars and propagandists are all sons and daughters of the West, namely, Madame Blavatsky, William Q. Judge, Col. Olcott, Dr. Mrs. Annie Besant, Bishop Leadbeater and Dr. Arundale.

All these Western thinkers made a deep study of the ancient teachings at their source. Nay, Madame Blavatsky, the great Russian genius and a spiritual soul of a rare order, spent her years in secret researches in the recesses and ruins of secluded Tibetan mountains, to gain personal experiences and knowledge of the arcane science. Her great psychic powers and super-abundant and intense desire to probe into the mysteries of nature for the benefit and lasting happiness of mankind, brought her into close touch with the supernormal agencies and her efforts were rewarded, through it meant considerable sacrifice. Her books *Isis Unveiled* and *The Secret Doctrine* are monumental volumes treating of the arcane science.

Theosophy is not a new revelation. It is the version of ancient teaching in a new and familiar garb, put forth in a language which contains no secret signs or symbols, no mystic hallucinations, no paradoxical quotations to allure the mind, no hierographic pigmentations or aberrations. It is a straight teaching of the Masters, the Great White Brotherhood of Adepts whose chief concern is to evolve and perfect this world of ours.

Theosophy is "sanctified common sense." Pure motive alone can not go a long way. It has to be allied with "wisdom." Theosophy is the path of wisdom. It is a blend of philosophy and religion. It is a science of Truth.

Universal Brotherhood is the fundamental teaching of the Theosophists. Theosophy has made a deep, comparative study of all the religions of the world and its findings that there is a remarkable unanimity in the fundamentals of all religions, even as regards *Karma* and re-incarnation, though some may refute such a statement, have solidified and clarified the whole position especially from the occult side of things. The teaching of the existence of the Masters as guiding and moulding the destinies of men and nations is another contribution of Theosophy to the modern world in its spiritual growth.

The chief motto of the Theosophist is "To be in the world, but not of the world," advocating thus an active, but detached life. In fact, the whole world, including even India, is now tending towards the teaching of a detached life of rigid activity as the best means of realizing

Truth. The old notion of passivity as an escape from the mire of *maya* is now being replaced with a healthier and more vital teaching of strenuous service without expectation of any return or reward.

"While doing the best you know in every act and present duty, do not attach yourself to any particular form of result. Leave results to the Law, — they will surely come in accordance with it. Having done your duty as you see it, resign all personal interest in the results. When ever the results, take them as that which your true self "really desired." Such is the teaching of Theosophy, namely to work without expectation of any return or reward to rise above our likes and dislikes, to be unconcerned of our own interest, to look upon every one as a link in life, to awaken spiritual consciousness at every step and every stage of life, to sacrifice, to deny and to ever seek to become ready for the Master, to make use of you as His organ, to spend the teaching of God's unity for the perfecting of the world.

Theosophy teaches two doctrines — the doctrine of the eye and the doctrine of the heart. The eye is the intellect; the heart is the spirit. Intellect is considered as the source of paramount power, but Theosophy like all other mystical and occult schools of thought, has convincingly proved that there is a force much greater than that of intellect and that is intuition, which is the force of spirit, the voice of the Masters, who expresses Himself through the vehicle of an aspirant after Truth.

C.W. Leadbeater says; "One intellect is a narrow thing —how limited no man realizes until he comes into touch with its higher developments, when he begins to see that the intellect about which we have boasted so much is in reality a poor affair, a beginning only, a seed of a future tree. In comparison to that of the future, men have now only a child-intellect, though it is that of a hopeful child, for it has done much already and shows promise of more. But compared with the intellect of the Great Ones it is still that of a very little child."

Intuition is the Buddhic faculty; it is the only means of obtaining Light of God. Printed words are only a ladder; they may indicate the way but self-realization can come only when we carry out the teachings of the Master which are infallible.

"From the unreal lead me to the Real,
From darkness lead me to Light,
From death lead me to Immortality."

This is the strain in which the Theosophist works for his own salvation and for the salvation of all mankind. Non-separateness is the keynote of the Theosophic teaching. It is the basis of the Theosophist's altruism.

It is said in the Bible, "*Enter ye in at the strait gate, for wide is the gate, and broad is the way, that leadeth to destruction, and many there be which go in thereat: Because strait is the gate and narrow is the way, which leadeth unto life and few there be that find it.*" (Matthew CH 7-13 and 14).

Theosophy in its exoteric and esoteric teachings is a great force in inducing men to leave the broad path which leads to destruction, so commonly followed by most of us in utter ignorance of the Divine Law and to turn to the narrow path, with a narrow gate for though it is as sharp and straight as a razor, it is nevertheless, the safest way. The narrow path is the path of God; it is the will of God. All of us sooner or later must eventually "enter into the stream." "For you are God and you will be only what God wills; but you must dig down into yourself, to find the God within you and listen to His voice, which is your voice."

Men should work as if to say that they are agents of God, carrying out His behests in every action of theirs. The unreal is that which is not divine, which has not the stamp of immortality, which is fluctuating and uncertain. The objects of the senses are unreal in this sense that they can not give us lasting satisfaction. God alone is Real. He dwells in the heart of every human being and it is by delving deep into its inner recesses that God-realization can be achieved.

"I know thou hast believed in Me
And life through Me is thine,
But where are all those glorious stars
Which in thy crown should shine?
Thou seest yonder joyous throng
With gems on every brow,
For every soul that led to Me,
They were a jewel now."

Every man according to Theosophic teaching is made up of body, soul and spirit. The word spirit which is derived from Latin *spiro*, means breath. The Spirit is the breath of God. The Theosophists call it Monad, the divine spark, which enters into the physical body, or rather say hovers round it, for the purpose of getting "definiteness and accuracy in material details." The plan of evolution, is that just as man is the crown of physical evolution, having evolved from the lower strata of existence, viz, the mineral, vegetable and animal kingdoms, he has also to ascend the higher spiritual realms by subduing the various bodies — the physical, the astral and mental of which he is composed. The soul which is only a part of the spirit has eventually to become absorbed in the spirit itself. The love of personality has to be crushed in order to give freedom to ego, which is the expression of the Monad. As Leadbeater says, "The evolution of the soul consists in its gradual return to the higher level on the plane next below the Nomadic carrying with it the result of its descent in the shape of the experiences gained and qualities acquired."

When the spirit and soul become one, it means unification of the ego with the Monad that is, achievement of man's goal in life, namely, attainment of Adeptship, the stage of the Superman. This final inclusion in the great hierarchy of the Adepts is the result of the co-operation of the man willing to serve the Master at any cost and sacrifice and of the Master teaching him the occult truths of the Mystic path. There is loving relationship between the accepted pupil and the Master, but it must be said that the Master's love for the pupil is not influenced, even in the slightest degree by any sense of attachment or favouritism. It is a love that is generated, when the Master feels that the accepted pupil is progressing spiritually for the attainment of the final goal. Ordinarily the evolution of the human soul will take many centuries but under the guidance of the Adepts, it is possible to achieve adeptship in the course of a few incarnations or births.

Poets are born, not made. We know of the instances of geniuses in various walks of life, but a natural born adept is something practically impossible. Every man or woman has to tread the rugged path of life, face calamities and sufferings, go through an ordeal of sacrifice, lead a rigid life of abstinence and purity, get mastery over all his vehicles, before he could be called upon to "enter into the stream." One has to lose himself completely before he can find God. Is it not Christ who said, "*He that findeth his life shall lose it: and he that loseth his life for My sake shall find it.*" (St. Matthew-Ch-X-39)

Complete devotion to his Master without expectation of any occult recognition is necessary for success in the occult path.

Leadbeater in his work, *The Master and the Path* gives the qualifications expected in a *chela* as mentioned in some ancient book, which are as under:

1) Perfect physical health.
2) Absolute mental and physical purity.
3) Unselfishness of purpose; universal charity, pity for all animate beings.
4) Truthfulness and answering faith in the law of *Karma*, independent of the intervention of any power in nature — a law whose course is not to be obstructed by any agency, not to be caused to deviate by prayer or propitiatory exoteric ceremonies.
5) A courage undaunted in every emergency even at peril of life.
6) An intuitional perception of one's being the vehicle of the manifested *Avalokiteshvara* or Divine Atma (spirit).
7) Calm indifference for, but just appreciation of, everything that constitutes the objective and transitory world in its relation with, and to, the invisible regions.

Leadbeater adds, "Such as least must have been the recommendations of one aspiring to perfect *chelaship.* With the sole exception of the first, which in rare and exceptional cases might have been modified each one of these points has been invariably insisted upon and all must have been more or less developed in the inner nature by the chela's *unhelpful* exertions before he could be actually put to the test." (Leadbeater's, *The Masters and the Path,* page 67).

Various religions and schools speak of the Mystic Path and the Mystic teachings. We have already referred to them in the preceding chapters of this book,—the teachings and commandments of Patanjali, the mystic and occult truths contained in that greatest of mystical works, the *Bhagawad Gita,* the philosophy of Shankaracharya, the school of *Hatha yoga,* which aims at purification by means of breathing exercises, *Raja yoga* the science of enkindling the serpent fire and various other schools and cults which speak of attainment of God-realization by means of meditation, *bhakti* and *mantras.* But so far as modern science is concerned, it must be stated that contribution of Theosophy in its teaching of the existence of the Masters is unique. We have already referred in the fore-going pages, to the monumental works of Madame Blavatsky,—not a profound scholar, but a mystic of the highest type, whose life affords the lesson of the greatest spiritual adventure in the world—we mean her *Secret Doctrine* and *Isis Unveiled.* Besides these two great works of immortal fame, she has written *The Voice of the Silence.*

Krishnamurti wrote, *At the Feet of the Master* at the early age of thirteen, under the inspiration of Master Kuthumi. The same Master had inspired Madame Blavatsky in her sublime work. *The Voice of the Silence. Light on the Path* is another Theosophical work of a highly Mystical nature. These three namely, *At the Feet of Master, The Voice of the Silence* and *The Light on the Path* form the steps or stages of the Mystic Path. *At the Feet of the Master* gives preparatory teaching to the candidate who wants to be initiated. *The Voice of the Silence* goes beyond the first initiation. It takes you right up to the fourth initiation, viz, the state of Arhatship. *The Light on the Path* is a very profound study leading up to the highest stage of Initiation,— the Mahachohan level. Both the latter are poetical.

An introspective review of these brilliant sages would not be out of place.

Krishnamurti was boldly young when he was chosen to become a vehicle for the Master's teaching. Dr. Annie Besant in writing a foreword to *At the Feet of the Master*, says, "The privilege is given to me as an elder to pen a word of introduction to this little book, the first written by a young brother, young in body verily, but not in soul."

In making the above remark, the learned author is expressing a great truth. A person's age is to be judged according to his or her evolving soul. In occult science the age is judged by the progress of the inner soul or the ego and not by the span of physical life.

The teachings contained in *At the Feet of the Master* were meant primarily by the great Master, who inspired the young boy to write, for his own personal benefit as he was being prepared for Initiation. What a tremendous awakening this small book must have created can be realized from the fact that it has been translated into 27 languages, that it has gone through more than forty editions, more than a hundred thousand copies have been sold off and a million copies were printed in America also. The boy author in his own preface says, "These are not my words; they are the words of the Master, who taught me. Without Him I could have done nothing ; but through His help I have set my feet upon the Path." And then the boy author appeals to others also to join the Path like him in the following words:

"You also desire to enter the Path, so the words which He spoke to me will help you also, if you will obey them. It is not enough to say that they are true and beautiful; a man who wishes to succeed must do exactly what is said. To look at food and say that it is good will not satisfy a starving man; he must put forth his hand and eat. So to hear the Master's words is not enough; you must do what he says, attending to every word, taking every hint."

"Waiting the word of the Master
Watching the Hidden Light:
Listening to catch His orders,
In the very midst of the fight;

Seeing His slightest signal,
Across the heads of the throne;
Hearing His faintest whisper
Above earth's loudest song."

The four qualifications that are mentioned which a candidate aspiring to tread the Path of Initiation must have are:

1) Discrimination
2) Desirelessness
3) Good Conduct
4) Love

Discrimination means opening the door of the mind. Hindus and Buddhists use the word "*viveka*" for discrimination. Christians call it "*conversion*". Says the Scripture, "*Set your heart on things above and not on things of the earth.*" "*For what shall it profit a man, if he shall gain the whole world, and lose his own soul.*"

(*St. Mark* Ch.-8-36)

Discrimination has to be practised by the pupil not only before he is permitted to enter the path, but at all stages of the path until its very end. It is the vision that makes him see what is real and what is unreal. It is not a man's religion, his label, his denomination that counts. It is the power to judge between right and wrong, it is the knowledge — the inner knowledge which has to be gained by man himself directly; it is the inner vision which he has to develop by the dint of his own faculties and experiences. "The really important thing is the knowledge — the knowledge of God's Plan for men. For, God has a plan and that plan is *evolution*. When a man has seen that and really knows it, he can not help working for it and making himself one with it because it is so glorious, so beautiful."

The plan of God's unity works so well in nature that he who thwarts it must suffer and he who goes in accordance with it taking himself to be a part of the whole, gains ground at every step and illumines not only his soul but illuminates the souls of others also and brings about peace and harmony so very necessary for the fruition of life's purpose. We must discard the ordinary mode of thinking which is based on separateness. "The One sees all."

"Why then squander time and money on selfish projects? The cause is invisible, but the effect is visible. We may not see God, but His presence is felt in the multiple diversity of His manifestation. The delusion is that we see things as different from Spirit. As the Gita says, "As a single sun illumines the whole world, even so does the embodied One illumine all bodies."

(*Bhagavad Gita* Ch XIII-33)

If this fundamental fact is grasped, that there is one Spirit, which pervades the universe, who is the Knower, the Perceiver, the Experiencer, there can be no separateness and no delusion.

True discrimination lies in following the path, according to this conception, that God is One, the Law is One and All are One. Authority, dogmatism, are the bane of spiritual progress. Freedom to exercise discrimination without interference of outside authority is essential in the path of spiritual advancement.

The second qualification is desirelessness.

It is said in the Vedas:

"The senses moving towards their appropriate objects, are producers of heat and cold, pleasure and pain, which come and go and are brief and changeable; these do not endure, O, son of Bharta. For the wise man, whom these disturb not and to whom pain and pleasure are the same is fitted for immortality. There is no existence for that which does not exist, nor is there any non-existence for what exists. By these, who see the truth and look into the principles of things, the ultimate characteristic of these both is seen."

(*Bhagavad Gita*—Ch.II-14, 15 and 16)

The word used in the Hindu Scriptures for desirelessness is "*vairagya*". It means renunciation. It is no doubt difficult to practise it. But when one gets the knowledge that God alone is Real and all else is *maya*, delusion, illusion, the craving for wealth and power, name and fame, dies away. They have no intrinsic value and they hamper the progress of the soul. As the Gita says, "The wise man is content with whatsoever cometh." He does not waste his time and energy on the gewgaws of life.

By desirelessness is meant not only renunciation. One should not even desire for heaven or release from re-birth.

Says the Master through the mouth of Alcyon, "Thus far all is simple, it needs only that you should understand. But there are some who forsake the pursuit of earthly aims only in order to gain heaven or to attain personal liberation from re-birth; into this error you must not fall."

The master wants desirelessness to be practised to such an extent that one should work not even for the purpose of gaining salvation but merely for the sake of work and helping the cause of human evolution. The Master says: "So you must do right for the sake of right, not in the hope of reward; you must work for the sake of work, not in the hope of seeing the result, you must give yourself to the service of the world, because you love it and cannot help giving yourself to it."

What God desires is that we must give un-stinted service to all, without expectation of any return or reward. This is the true renunciation and not that of the *sanyasi*, who leaves the domestic home to lead a life in the solitude of the forest or the mountain cave for his own liberation.

The desire for psychic powers is also not authorised by the Master unless they are freely given to aid the aspirant in his work of doing good to mankind. The astral eye which is known by the name of "clairaudience" are psychic gifts.

The Master says,"Have no desires for psychic powers, but they will come when the Master knows that it is best for you to have them."

The above lines are significant and it is absurd to run down Spiritualism and Psychism, *ad hoc*. One should not crave for psychic powers, but when they come naturally, they are meant to be used for higher purposes and they must be accepted without fear of consequences. Bishop Leadbeater says, "It is wisdom to use to the full the powers one has and to have no desires for psychic powers until the Master sees fit that we should develop them."

Leadbeater was a clairvoyant of the highest type and he has written many works on Spiritualism, taking a very fair stand and his liberal and just attitude deserves commendations. The following passage deserves to be widely read, by the Theosophists themselves in the first instance as they are inclined to run down Spiritualism and Psychism without a proper understanding of the whole situation. In fact, I was myself a victim of the anger of the local Theosophists, when I wrote a series of articles which appeared in a local journal, some years ago. Says Leadbeater: "The Masters influence many people and care nothing about whether the instruments they use know them or not; therefore, we must be prepared to find that quite outside Theosophical organizations other forces are working towards the same great goal. And while we follow our line and serve our own society firmly, strongly, faithfully, loyally, keeping to that because it is obviously the way for us, yet we should be careful not to condemn or to speak against any other forms of manifestation outside it which may be tending in the same general direction and we must not expect such manifestations to be all pure and perfect. In all sorts of ways spiritual power will be out-poured from now on to the time of the coming. The Hierarchy itself is pouring upon the world floods of influence which may perhaps touch but very little the man who is entirely wrapt up in wordly matters but which mean a great deal to those who are sensitive; to those who are ready to profit by it; it will mean the making of a new heaven and a new earth." (*Talks on the Path of Occultism*- Vol 1 pages 141 and 142)

It must be remembered that whatever power a man has obtained, whether psychic or not psychic, if it is used for the benefit *of others* no harm can at all come to the user. Christ says, "Unto every one that hath shall be given and he shall have abundance; but from him that hath not shall be taken away even that which he hath."

Leadbeater interpreting the above allegorical teaching of Christ says: "He who uses his powers to the full shall be entrusted with more; he who does not use his powers and who therefore from the occult point of view does not possess them shall lose even the possibility of using them; they will atrophy."

The only touchstone and the key is your own altruism. If your nature is pure and sincere and your desire is to serve mankind, the possession of psychic powers is a beneficial gift, poured unto you by the beneficent influence of the Masters, who know how to make us of their instruments for the evolution of mankind.

The third qualification is good conduct. All the religions of the world have spoken so profusely of the necessity of good conduct in life, that it would be superfluous to deal with the subject so commonly known to every one. But the Master puts an emphasis on certain traits in human character which are necessary for control of the mind. They are as under:-

1) Self control in thought.
2) Self control in action.
3) Tolerance.
4) Cheerfulness.

5) One pointedness.
6) Confidence.

Prejudices, irritations, outbursts of anger, jealousies, selfishness — these are enemies of mental tranquillity. Tolerance, cheerfulness, a sense of humour, concentration and confidence are the *satwic* properties, which create mental harmony and a feeling of inner joyousness, which bring us nearer to the realization of God. Courage is another trait of character, which every aspirant must develop. As Dr. Besant says,"It has its root in a recognition of the unity of Self." Thc aspirant is usually molested and all sorts of accusations and calumnies are poured upon his devoted head. But he must brave the onslaught and not allow his mind to be disturbed in any way.

Says the Master: "It does not matter in the least what happens to a man from the outside: sorrows, troubles, sicknesses, losses — all these must be as nothing to him and must not be allowed to affect the calmness of his mind. They are the results of past actions and when they come you must bear them cheerfully, remembering that all evil is transitory and that your duty is to remain always joyous and serene. They belong to your previous lives, not to this; you can not alter them, so it is useless to trouble about them."

All sorrows and trials must eventually pass away, but the good we do and the progress we achieve in the inner consciousness of our heart remain for ever. Every time that we suffer quietly, we not only reduce the heavy load of past *karma*, but we sow the seeds of permanent bliss hereafter.

Leadbeater says, "It has often been pointed out that a man can take over from life to life, in his causal body, only his good qualities. This is quite true. The causal body, is constructed from the matter of higher sub-planes of the mental plane — the first, second and third and the matter of these levels can not vibrate in response to any of the lower or less desirable qualities. Therefore a man can actually build into himself only good, which is very fortunate for us, because otherwise we should all have built in a great deal that is not good, which would retard our evolution instead of helping it. But he carries over with him the permanent atoms belonging to the different planes — mental, astral and physical — and so the vibrations which belong to them come up as inherent, qualities in his new vehicles." (Talks on the Path of Occultism Vol I, page 100) Study is essential for the progress of the soul but it should be not for self-gratification but for the purpose of serving humanity in some form or other.

One of the greatest superstitions is the importance given by the so-called religious minded to rites and ceremonies. The words of the Master in this respect are very significant. They speak of the necessity of observing tolerance in such regard. The Master says, "You must learn that no ceremonies are necessary; else you must part of your nature that you follow it without needing to think of it and can not turn aside. You, the Monad have decided it, to break away from it would be to break away from yourself."

The last injunction of the Master to the boy Krishnamurti is, "You must trust your Master. You must trust yourself. If you have seen the Master, you will trust Him to the uttermost through many lives and deaths. If you have not yet seen Him, you must still try to realize Him and trust Him, because if you do not, even He cannot help you."

The Master further says: "You must trust yourself. You say, you know yourself too well. If you feel so, you do not know yourself: you only know the weak outer husk which has fallen often in the mire. But you, the real you — you are a spark of God's own fire and God who is Almighty is in you and because there is nothing that you can not do, if you will. Say to yourself: What man has done, man can do. I am a man, yet also God in man. I can do things and I will." "For your will must be like tempered steel, if you would tread the path."

The fourth qualification is Love. Love is divine. It is immortal. Its wings cover everything. But the word used here is the intense desire on the part of the pupil for unification with God, which is the goal of life. The great Buddha taught us of *nirvana* and this is possible of attainment by means of love for all beings sentient or insentient. Love is the dispeller of hatred; it is the ointment of the soul. It is spiritual balm. It is the summit of altruism. It is the gateway of the life eternal.

Let us now cast a glance on Madame *Blavatsky's Voice of the Silence.* In occultism we always meet paradoxical phrases. "Silence" and "Voice" connote opposite meanings, but there is a depth of significance in the title. God is silence. His voice reigns supreme in the human heart and to hear that voice is to commune with the Divinity, which is all Bliss.

But the question is, how to hear that voice ? The first thing essential, says the Master is to slay the mind, which acts as a barrier between the soul and spirit.

"The mind is the great Slayer of the Real
Let the discipline slay the slayer."

"The soul rocks between the two opposing waves of delusion and reality. Says the Master: "When to the world's turmoil thy budding soul lends ear; when to the roaring voice of the great illusion thy soul responds; when frightened the sight of the hot tears of pain, when deafened by the cries of distress, thy soul withdraws like the shy turtle within the carapace of selfhood, learn, O, disciple of her silent God, thy soul is an unworthy shrine."

But if the soul conquers *maya* and enters into the Hall of Wisdom, it obtains the wings of omniscience. It becomes the altar of compassion. It listens to the cry of every pain and sheds its tears in sympathy. "These tears, O thou of heart most merciful, these are the streams that irrigate the fields of charity immortal. 'Tis on such soil that grows the midnight blossom of Buddha more difficult to find more rare to view than is the flower Vogay tree. It is the seed of freedom from rebirth. It isolates the Arhat both from strife and lust, it leads him through the fields of being into the peace and bliss known only in the land of silence and non-being."

It is said between the First and Fifth Initiation about fourteen rounds of births are taken, which looking to the fact, that hundreds even thousands of lives are spent before the person is admitted for initiation is comparatively a short span. When the soul reaches the Fourth Initiation i.e., it becomes an Arhat, it enters the nirvanic plane.

"And now, rest' neath the Bodhi tree, which is perfection of all knowledge for, know thou art the master of *Samadhi*—the state of faultless vision.

Behold ! thou hast become the light, thou has become the sound, thou art thy Master and thy God. Thou art thyself the object of thy search: the voice unbroken, that resounds through out eternities, exempt from change, the seven sounds in one, the Voice of the Silence. *Aum Tat Sat.*"

The above lines indicate that the true Bodhisattva refuses to accept the nirvana bliss and makes this renunciation for the purpose of serving humanity.

"To reach Nirvana's bliss but to renounce it, is the supreme, the final step — the highest on renunciation's path."

The last and highest stage is that of Adeptship. When an Initiate becomes an Adept, he remains aloof but at the same time he has all the powers of even descending to the physical plane for the duty allotted to the members of the White Lodge is primarily to evolve the world, which they do in a hundred fold manner, being endowed with vaster consciousness and powers.

THE ADEPTS

The fulcrum of Theosophical teaching is the Law of Evolution. It is God's plan, that man must by his own self-induced and self-devised efforts unfold the powers latent in him and become a Buddha, a Christ, which is in him. He is aided in his efforts by a Hierarchy of a Higher Order, when the time comes. This Hierarchy is known in the Theosophical parlance as the White Lodge of the Brotherhood of Adepts. They are perfected Men, Spiritualised individuals Mahatmas. Adeptship is the last stage in the evolution of the human soul.

Man is liberated and perfected. He achieves tremendous powers, which are used again for the evolution of the world. For, it is God's Plan, that the exiled soul, descending into matter must get liberated from the wheel of birth and death and returning to the original source, get absorbed into the universal.

As a theory, it sounds very well. Every religion teaches us of the goal of life. The founders of religion were perfected souls —Zoroaster, Lord Krishna, Buddha, Jesus, Moses and Mohammed. But religions do not carry us further. Theosophy on the contrary has rent the veil. The existence of the Perfected Men, "is one of the most important of the many new facts which Theosophy puts before us." Dr. Besant in her several spirited lectures has given her own testimony and that of her various other Theosophical friends of the fact of the existence of the Hierarchy of Adepts, watching, guiding and helping the evolution of men. Leadbeater's book, *The Masters and the Path* gives a graphic account of the existence of the Masters. In fact, the foundation of the Theosophic Society is the outcome of the bidding of the Masters.

Madame Blavatsky has been accused by the ignorant, as a fraud, a charlatan. She was the first to have contacted the Masters, when she was in Tibet. It was through the Masters, that she got all the materials of the ancient religious books and Scriptures which she welded into one whole and gave to the world her monumental work, *The Secret Doctrine.* Madame Blavatsky was a woman of fervent intellect, frank, out-spoken, sincere, capable of laborious study, but by no means such a profound scholar, as could have produced by means of her own knowledge such an epoch-making if not original work as *The Secret Doctrine.* It is true as the accusers say that the book is not original but the accusation that she can not claim merit as she borrowed all her materials from the various scriptures and ancient books is not correct. In a very relevant rejoinder Dr. Besant exposes the hollowness of the argument of the critics, and we reproduce it here.

"But what you have to consider is this: that she never claimed that she discovered the knowledge she gave to the world; that her contention is that this knowledge comes down from a far off past; is found in every scripture, in every philosophy; and the very purpose of that book is to quote from every direction, from the scriptures of every religion, from the writings of every people, in order to show the identity of the teaching and to prove the antiquity of the doctrine. What is new in this book is not what has been said by Orientalists and may be pointed to in one or another sacred book of the world. What is new is the knowledge which enabled her to select from the whole of these the facts which build up a single mighty conception of the evolution of the universe, the evolution of man, the coherent synthesis of the whole cosmogony.

"And that is her title to be the greatest Teacher of our time, because she had real knowledge and not mere book learning, knowledge which enabled her to collect from scattered books the truth which fitted together, made one mighty whole, because she held the clue which she was able to follow with unerring accuracy through the maze and show that all the scattered materials contained within them the possibility of the single building. And her work is the more wonderful because she did it not being a scholar; because she did it not having had the education which could have enabled her to some extent to piece this knowledge together; because she did it what no Orientalists have done with all their learning; what not all the Orientalists together have done with all the help of their knowledge of Eastern tongues and their study of Eastern literature.

"There is not one of them who out of that tangled mass brought out that mighty synthesis; not one of them out of that chaos was able to build up a cosmos. But this Russian woman who with little education, this Russian woman who was no scholar, and pretended to be none, somewhere or other she gained a knowledge that enabled her to do what none of your scholars can do; somewhere or the other she had a teaching which enabled her to reduce this chaos to order and to bring out in a mighty scheme of evolution, which makes us understand the universe and man. She said it was not hers; she never claimed to have originated it; she was always speaking of her own want of knowledge and referring to Those who taught her."

We have quoted the above long passage from Dr. Mrs. Annie Besant's work, *The Masters,* so that the readers may realize the wantonness of the accusation and the unanswerable manner in which Dr. Besant, the brilliant co-worker of Madame Blavatsky, exposed the false charges. We would refer our reader to Dr. Besant's other work. *H.P. Blavatsky and The Masters of Wisdom,* in which the brilliant author gives a graphic account of the victimisation of Madame Blavatsky and the false report issued by the Psychic Research Society based on the investigations of one of its members — Mr. Hodgson.

That the existence of the Masters is a fact is verified by the testimony of several persons, who had come into contact with them. Leadbeater gives a list of the names of the Masters contacted by him and others. He says, "There is a considerable amount of personal testimony. Madame Blavatsky and Colonel Olcott, the co-founders of the Theosophical Society, Dr. Annie Besant, our present President and I myself — all of us have seen some of these great ones and many other members of the Society have also been privileged to see one or two of them and there is ample testimony in what all these people have written." The Masters mentioned in the Theosophical literature, as guiding the destiny of the world are Master Morya, Master Kuthumi, Master Djwal Kul, Prince Rakoczy, Master Jesus and Master Hilarion. Master Hilarion who wears a Cretan body and lives mostly in Egypt inspired Madame Blavatsky to write *The Voice of the Silence* and M.C. to write *Light on the Path*. Master Morya and Master Kuthumi more known as K.H., were the two Masters who according to Sinnet founded the Theosophical Society through the instrumentality of Col. Olcott and Madame Blavatsky. They also inspired Sinnet to write his work, *Esoteric Buddhism*, which to speak in the words of Dr. Annie Besant "brought the light of Theosophy to thousands in the West." Both the above Masters live mostly in Tibet, using Indian bodies. Masters Rakoczi who travels much, lives mostly in Hungary. He is called the "Hungarian Adept." Master Jesus lives in the mountains of Lebanon. The other Adepts are, "The Venetian" and "Serapis" who taught Col. Olcott for some time.

It must be said that the Adepts are free citizens of space. The whole universe is their home. They can discard and put on whatever vehicles they want, as necessities arise, whether physical, astral or mental. They live at their highest. They were men in flesh and blood, before they reached the Adeptship. Leadbeater says, "They tell us with one accord that no long time ago, they stood where we now stand. They have risen out of the ranks of ordinary humanity and they have told us that we in time to come shall be as they are now and that the whole system is a graded evolution of Life extending up and up, further than where we can follow it, even unto the Godhead itself."

This physical world is the training school for the ego. It is a world of struggle against evil created by man himself in his ignorance. If he succeeds in slaying his passions and become master of himself, he passes out and enters into the life of Reality — into the life of the Spirit. It is our selfishness that prevents us from unfolding the powers latent in us for the emancipation of the soul and realization of that glory and that power which is the marked goal of every soul and which each soul must eventually must reach whether in a hundred births or a thousand births. 'Humanity is the final class of the world school.' The Adept is the flower of the Perfected man, the consummation of God's plan of evolution.

The Adepts live for others. In this world of ours, self forms chiefly the basis of our activity. Among the Adepts, absolute non-selfishness is the key of their activity. Their powers are exceedingly wide. Their consciousness knows no bound. They have eliminated their lower self completely and they work strenuously, day in and day out, 'in helping forward evolution.' They work in harmony with the Logos who guide and directs them. They take pupils, when they are satisfied, that they will progress spiritually and can reach the final goal viz, nirvana or adeptship.

The work of the Adepts is to pour their spiritual force for the advancement of religious, moral, intellectual and economic condition of human beings. As Dr. Besant says, "They aid in countless ways, the progress of humanity." Just as the sun throws its light and purifies the earth, the Adepts make use of the human beings, ripe for spiritual progress by inspiring them to carry out God's Plan of mighty evolution. Leaders in political, social literary and religious fields receive inspiration from the members of the Great Brotherhood and with their help, they mould and shape the destiny of all mankind. These Adepts are continuously busy in nullifying the evil currents in life and they pour out their thought forms of love and virtue for the good of all humanity. They work strenuously for bringing amity and peace. As Dr. Annie Besant says "They stand a guardian wall around humanity, within which it can progress uncrushed by the tremendous comic forces, which play around our planetary house. From time to time one of them comes forth into the world of men, as a great religious teacher, to carry on the task of spreading a new form of the Eternal Verities, a form suitable to a new race or civilisation. Their ranks include all the greatest prophets of the Faiths of the world and while a religion lives, one of these great Ones is ever at its head, watching over it as His special charge." (Dr. Besant's *The Masters.* pages 63 and 64.)

The Masters are the highest products of evolution. To doubt their existence is futile. There was a time, when sceptics ridiculed the very idea of their existence. But thanks to Theosophy; this divine science has amply manifested that the existence of the Masters, is as natural; as the flowers that blossom in the garden and the sun that throws its radiant light on the earth beneath; ripening the corn in the fields. The Masters are the fragrant flowers and ripened fruit of the labours of men, flung over centuries of struggle carried on in this mundane world. The way to Adeptship is open to all. Those who shall seek it shall find it. This reminds us of the Biblical truth "*Ask, and it shall be given you; seek, and ye shall find; knock, and it shall be opened unto you.*" (Mathew Ch. 7-7)

The whole Theosophic ideology is based on the conception of the Masters, variously called as Adepts, Mahatmas, *Elders* Members of the White Lodge Brotherhood. When Madame Blavatsky was accused of fraud, she said she was ready to sacrifice her life, so exalted was her soul, so beautiful her spirit, but what she strongly resented and protested against, was that if such an accusation were to go unchallenged, it would mean the Society's death, for, "T.S. minus Masters., is an absurdity." What this brave woman has suffered deserves to be enshrined in the hearts of all true men and women and her name written on the Scroll of Eternity. The following is an affectionate tribute paid by Dr. Annie Besant to the Memory of this heroic woman:

"What H.P. Blavatsky was, the world may some day know. She was of heroic stature and smaller souls instinctively resented her strength, her titanic nature. Unconventional, careless of appearances, frank to unwisdom — as the world estimates wisdom — too honest to calculate against dishonesty of others; she laid herself open to continual criticism and misunderstanding. Full of intellectual strength and with extraordinary knowledge, she was humble as a little child. Brave to recklessness, she was pitiful and tender. Passionately indignant when accused of sins she loathed, she was generous and forgiving to a repentant foe. She had a hundred splendid virtues and a few petty failings. May the Master she served with unfaltering courage, with unwavering devotion send back to us again the Brother you know as H.P.B., but we — otherwise."

It is said that there are fifty to sixty Supermen — adepts that are working in harmony for the evolution of the entire world. Their number is small, but they have so arranged their work, that they have taken into consideration every bit of life, discarding nothing as negligible. The Church in the olden times used to so divide its work, that even the remotest villages had parish priests. In the same manner, the adepts have divided their work and nothing escapes their vision or vigilance. They wield their control not on small areas but large continents. They control not only human evolution but they are vigilant and watchful of all activities in all kingdoms. They not only inspire men; they inspire even angels. They guard the nature spirits. They look after the various kingdoms, the animal, the mineral and the vegetable. They control also the kingdoms of the elemental essence and various other bodies of which we are not even aware of.

When wars break out and catastrophes take place on earth, such as fire, famine and flood, we should not in our ignorance attribute them to the doings of the Adepts. It is a mistake to do so. Every nation has its *karma*, just as an individual has his *karma* to be fulfilled and the only thing with which the adepts can not interfere is the working of the Karmic Law. All that the Great Hierarchy can do is to loosen its beneficent forces of love and compassion, in a larger measure and thus try to retrieve the extent of misery.

It may also be mentioned that the Adepts do the work of guarding human souls when they leave this physical plane for the non-physical. They play the role of ministering angels at a very critical moment when the departing souls need all the guidance in the new planes of existence.

The work of the Adept falls within the scheme and plan of the Logos. Leadbeater says, "All this is part of the scheme of the Logos, who apparently has calculated upon our taking part in His plan. When He devised it He thought: 'When my people shall rise to a certain level, they will begin to co-operate intelligently with me; therefore I shall arrange so that when they come to the point they will be able to draw open my power.' Thus He is counting upon every one."

The Adept is a spirit guide to millions of egos in this life. He is daily nay hourly passing out His resplendent rays of wisdom, cheer and helpfulness in abundance and they penetrate into millions of human cell. They create simultaneous awakening.

Says Leadbeater: "Each of the Adepts who have undertaken this special work is raying out upon enormous numbers of people, running often into many millions simultaneously; and yet such is the wonderful quality of this power which He pours forth, that it adapts itself to each one of these millions as though he were the only object of its influence, and it appears as though what for us would be full attention were given to that one."

(Leadbeater's *The Masters and the Path*, page 352)

The Adept has also to deal with many special cases and for this part of work, he appoints *devas*; to carry it out on his behalf, giving them liberty of action, within well defined limits. The *devas* in their turn employ nature spirits and thus the work of evolution is carried on through many agencies, each working under the guidance of the superior agency and of all the agencies, God alone is the Master and the Controller.

Wherever there are congregations, religious ceremonies, the Adepts pour their beneficent rays of helpfulness. The religious ceremonies and congregations make an easy channel for receiving the Adept's outpourings of His heart for man's moral and spiritual progress. The Adepts never miss any opportunity of sending their rays of joy and cheer. They are the Invisible Helpers. They make the receptive minds of men the channels for the flow of the life giving nectar of their spiritual energy and power.

Leadbeater concludes his book: "*The Masters and the Path*" with a most fervid statement, which is so full of splendour and human appeal, that we can not but reproduce it here for the benefit of our readers:

The Goal of All

"Far above us as is all the splendour of these great heights at present, it is worth our while to lift our thought towards them and try to realize them a little. They show the goal before every one of us, and the clearer our sight of it the swifter and steadier will be our progress towards it, though we may not all hope to fulfil the ancient ideal in this, and fly as an arrow to the mark.

In the course of this great progress every man will some day reach full consciousness on the highest of our planes, the Divine Plane and be conscious simultaneously at all levels at the *Prakritic* Cosmic plane, so that having in himself the power of the highest, He shall yet be able to comprehend and function on the very lowest, and help where help is needed. That omnipotence and omnipresence surely await every one of us and though this lower life may not be worth living, that we may gain from it for ourselves, yet it is magnificently worth enduring as a necessary stage for the true life that lies before us. 'Eye hath not seen, not ear heard, neither hath it entered into the heart of man to conceive the things which God hath prepared for them that love Him', for the love of God, the wisdom of God, the power of God, and the glory of God pass all understanding, even as does His peace."

16

Nature Mysticism

Nature is a source of great attraction to those whose souls are attuned with God. Artists and poets especially adore nature. It does not necessarily mean that they are all nature mystics. It is a question whether we would call a man like Lord Byron, a nature mystic. This man with infinite talent for poesy, — a man of great and fervid imagination — sought nature, to snatch moments of solace to soothe his afflicted mind and nerves. Some of the most beautiful, poetical passages in Byron's works are the result of his exultation in the awe and beauty of nature. The description of the "Ocean" in *Child Harold* is a classical piece by itself. His description of the mountain scenery of the Alps in *Manfred*, shows how his melancholy soul loves to wander over the vast vistas of nature to find a cure for the deadly inward grief. Nature is a nurse, an asylum, a soother to men like Byron, highly strung in nerves, with a mind vivid and active and a heart throbbing to imbibe the juice of nature, to soothe and nurse the overwrought body, wounded by the tempests of passion.

To poets like Wordsworth, nature is a teacher, a harmoniser, a beautifier and an inspirer. Nature is a grand mirror reflecting God's beauty to those who are in tune with God. The green trees and the chirping birds, the grey mountains with their snowy tops and the gliding rivers, the deep ravines and sunlit meadows, the flowers that throw their fragrance in the air and the bushes that shine with the lustre of the rising sun, are all God's messengers, embodiments of truths scattered all round, breathing an atmosphere of harmony and music and creating that resplendent Beauty, which is God.

Plato talked of Goodness, Beauty, Truth. Nature is symbolic of those virtues. It is only the mystic that understands this symbolic garb of God. Nature is a veil spread over the reality to the one whose soul is not open to God-consciousness. But to the real mystic, nature is no illusion. His inward eyes can behold the working of nature behind the outward phenomena of colour and form. Just as in a piece of tapestry of line and colour, what supports it is the warp and the woof inwardly hidden, so, in nature, what is hidden is God, who is the cause of harmony, order, beauty, rhythm and joy. To the mystic mind this force behind nature becomes apparent and his soul exhilarates in its charm and beauty. Take these lines of Wordsworth which he wrote on visiting the small river Wye:

"Therefore am I still
A lover of the meadows and the woods,
And mountains; and of all that we behold
From this green earth, of all the mighty world
Of eye and ear — both what they half create;
And what perceive; well pleased to recognise
In nature and the language of the sense,
The anchor of my purest thoughts, the nurse,
The guide, the guardian of my heart and soul;
Of all my moral being.

What a glorious tribute to nature ! This is the feeling which over 'powers those of us of kindred spirit. Nature creates a sense of joy and beauty and from one vision of beauty we pass on to another till we reach the vision of God Himself, — the flight of the Alone to the Alone. We feel an insight into the divine, we feel a mysterious joy, a thrilling sensation so beautifully described by Wordsworth in the following lines:

"that blessed mood,
In which the burthen of the mystery,
In which the heavy and weary weight —
Of all this unintelligible world,
In which the affections gently lead us on,
Until the breath of the corporeal frame,
And even the motion of our human blood,
Almost suspended, we are laid asleep,
In body and become a living soul.
While with an eye made quiet by the power
Of harmony, and the deep power of joy,
We see into the life of things."

What a fine mystical passage? We have said that to the mystic nature is not only a soother, an inspirer, but also a teacher. Even common-place things to the mystic mind acquire great importance and become the source of great inspiration. How beautifully Wordsworth says:

"To me the meanest flower that blows can give
Thoughts that do often lie too deep for tears."

Eekbart says, "The more God is in all things, the more He is outside them. The more He is within, the more without." What is meant is that God is both transcendental and immanent and when we look at nature, we feel the same sensation. He is immanent in every tree and bush, in every leaf and flower, in every meadow and glen, in every mountain and valley, in the breeze that blows and the cloud that rolls on, in the sea that murmurs the music of the waves and the sun that rises in the sky and throws its resplendent and life giving rays on the earth below. A feeling of joy comes when our soul unites with the soul of nature. But God is transcendent also. To the nature mystic who looks at Him in this light, God's vision creates awe and reverence. He always thinks of Him as something, "Yonder, Yonder."

Many of our mystic saints have learnt their first lessons in mysticism, by imbibing the inspiration of nature. St. Bernard said, "What I know of the divine sciences and holy scriptures, I learnt in woods and fields. I have had no other masters than beaches and oaks." And in another of his letters he says, "Listen to a man of experience: thou wilt learn more in the woods than in books. Trees and stones will teach thee more than thou canst acquire from the mouth of a magister."

> The same thought is expressed by Wordsworth when he says:
> "One impulse from the vernal wood
> Will tell you more of man,
> Of moral evil and of good,
> Than all the sages can."

Among the nature mysties of the modern times may be mentioned the following names: Carlyle, Emerson, Tennyson, Wordsworth, William Blake, William Morris, Mathew Arnold. The nature mystic is an idealist with a love for beauty and refinement. He is a reformer whose soul hungers for refashioning of things, surrounding him, so as to conform to the beauty of the soul within. He is an inspirer, though he may lack in executive ability. He is a dreamer, an artist, who weaves beautiful patterns and brings light and sunshine into the shoddy byways of life.

William Blake, a great artist and poet is considered to be one of the finest modern nature mystics. This is how he sings:

> "I will not cease from mental strife,
> Nor shall my soul fall from my hand,
> Till I have built Jerusalem,
> Within this green and pleasant land!"

The nature mystics are Jerusalem builders — builders of beautiful cities, where love and concord reign supreme and wisdom is the guardian angel.

C. Jinrajdasa, the present President of the Theosophical Society in the course of a very learned treatise on "The Nature of Mysticism" considers the fundamental basis of Buddhism as a "Nature Mysticism," of a unique type. Buddhism does not believe in a personal God. It is because of the absence of such a conception that it is erroneously classified as Atheism, which is absurd. What Buddha taught was that the whole universe is a vast Becoming and he laid down the great Law, "irresistible and imperishable," — that which he called *Dhamma*, the Sanskrit equivalent for which is *Dharma*. Now this Law is not revelation of God. "It is purely a statement of true relation between things as they eternally are," as Jinrajdasa put it. It is not a mere abstraction but a living power that pervades nature, whose centre is Love. When we meditate upon nature, we are meditating according to Buddha on the working of this great Law, — the Law of Cause and Effect. This Law according to Buddha is the gate way to Salvation. It is man's refuge and the way to purification, leading to nirvana. This is what Buddha says about the Law:

"Its effects are immediate, it is unlimited by time, it is conducive to salvation, it invites all comers, it is the fitting object of contemplation, the wise ponder it in their hearts."

Buddha's great teaching, "Hatred ceaseth not by hatred, hatred ceaseth only by love" is akin to Christ's great teaching of Love as the paramount power in realizing God. And what is Mysticism, if not love — love of God, man and nature.

17

The Spirit's Final Triumph

As we are now drawing to the end of our work, it would not be wrong to sum up the conclusions which the reader must have arrived at from the perusal of the preceding pages.

Mysticism is the topmost mast of humanity, it is its blossoming flower, the highest and the best in human ideology. It is the soul's treasure; nay the final triumph of the spirit. The mystic realizes the fundamental laws in nature, the Laws of Evolution. He knows that in the infinity of time and space, cause and effect are the same. The seed of effect is in the cause and the seed of cause is in the effect. The tyro beginner asked the question whether the egg came first or the hen. The simple reply is that the egg was contained in the hen and the hen in the egg. Both existed together.

In the similar manner God is in all and all is in God. Nothing exists without God. We have already explained that God is a cosmic force, divine fire, and every *jeeva*—individual soul—is a spark of that divine force or fire. The ultimate object of the divine plan is that this spark should re-unite with the parental fire just as a drop of water slips into the ocean and is merged into it. We have already shown that the way to the Absolute is through the path of renunciation, intensification of love for God and dedication of one's life to human service. In the path of *yoga*, individuality has to be suppressed. The self has to become non-self. When that is achieved, the crown of victory can be worn. Madame Blavatsky says: "Merge personality in the ego and the ego in the Monad and thereby become One with the universal ALL."

This final triumph of the spirit is described in a Tibetan hand book, in a very descriptive manner:

"Where is thy individuality lanoo? Where is the lanoo himself? It is the spark lost in the fire, the drop within the ocean, the ever present ray become the All and the Eternal Radiance." (*Voice of the Silence*)

Two questions arise from the contemplation of the above cosmic truth. First, why God at all should have allowed the sparks of its fire to emanate from it, which has resulted in so much of misery and degradation on the earthly plane ? God is all radiant and glorious and beautiful. We see this radiance as we watch the course of the seasons and look at the blue sky, the towering mountains and the gliding rivers, the humming brooks and the waving trees, the chirping birds and the many coloured rainbow. Why in the midst of such gorgeous splendour of the universe, man is placed to battle with filth, squalor, degradation and empty illusions? Why should man who emanates from God sin and suffer? The mystic understands the plan of God. It is the Law of Evolution.

God is spoken of in the scriptures as Unmanifest Absolute, without beginning, without end. It was a joyous sacrifice on the part of the Absolute to manifest Himself and the Law of Evolution working in the physical as well as spiritual realms is the outcome of that manifestation.

The word is God: the Law is God. And this Law has to be followed and obeyed.

Man suffers because he has to go through the phase of purification, to get rid of the bodily attachment, which is an obstacle in the path of the final triumph of the spirit — the liberation of the soul.

This process of evolution may be called the *Leela* or the sport of God, though it must be understood that it gives no enjoyment to God, to see His children suffer. The mystic understands that the whole creation is the result of divine plan and the suffering of man is caused not by divine action but that it is the outcome of man's wrongful use of his free will. But eventually he must reach God, though it may mean cycles of births and deaths. In the case of a few, *jivan mukti* is obtained in the course of a few incarnations. It all depends upon the individual's effort to follow the right couse, as directed by his own intutition, which is the guidance derived from the experiences of past lives. But why God should have created the Law and subjected man to suffering before he could be re-united with Him in the final stage of his perfection, is more than we can say. It is beyond the scope of human understanding.

The second question is that some day or the other the Law of Evolution must work itself out and all human beings will become evolved souls fit to be merged in God, which is said to be the object of the divine plan. In that case what else would be left to be done in the cosmic order of things? This again is beyond our human comprehension.

God is beginningless, endless. His universe is endless. Time and space are endless. We are concerned with the evolution of our own soul and this is possible as the mystics say, by leading a unitive life, a life of purity and non-attachment and non-separateness. The union of the inner mind with the universal Mind is the object of life. This goal appears visionary but the declaration of the mystics who have attained *nirvana* and ultimate union with God are so emphatic that we must feel convinced of the possibility of the divine *yoga*.

Patanjali, one of the greatest mystics of the ancient time, who is the author of the *Yoga Shutras* speaks of the eight limbs of the *yoga*. They are *Yama, Niyama, Asana, Pranayama, Pratyahara. Dharana, Dhyana* and *Samadhi*. In the Egyptian mysteries, the initiate is allowed to enter the inner temple only after he has passed the stage of purification. So also in the Hindu system, *Yama* and *Niyama* are the purifying elements. *Ahimsa* (non-injury) Truth, nonstealing, *Brahmacharya* (continence) and non-possession — these constitute *yama*. Purity, contentment, penance, study of scriptures and surrender to God, — these constitute *Niyama*.

Asana is a mechanical process of purification. So may be called *Pranayama*, which is the control of the breath. *Pratyahara* is the control of the mind which is a difficult thing and the most important in the practice of yoga. No person however good and religious, he may be, will ever be able to realize God, unless he meditates. Meditation is the be-all and end-all of the spiritual life. Righteousness alone is not enough. The mystic understands that it is by the way of concentrated thought, meditation and profound contemplation, that he can rise to the stage of perfection of the soul, — the flight of the alone to the Alone. In English, "concentratd thought" "meditation" and "deep contemplation" mean one and the same thing but the Sanskrit words used in the Hindu Scriptures viz *Dharana, Dhyana* and *Samadhi* constitute three distinct and varying stages of meditation. Dharana is the first stage, *Dhyana* is the second and *Samadhi* is the third stage. The last is the highest stage of bliss, when the meditator loses entire consciousness, as meditator, meditation and the object of meditation are fused into one viz, the object of meditation.

Meditation and non-separateness form the warp and woof of the structure of the mystic's life. Will power and intense love for God, which expresses itself again in human love and selfless service, are the two wings of the mystic in the flight of the alone to the Alone.

The general notion is that the mystic is non-active. Meditation appears to be inaction. But really speaking it is not so. It is the most active form of work. But leaving aside the controversy whether the mystics are active or passive, the tendency of the modern times requires mystics of the active brand. In ancient India, it used to be the practice of those in search of God, to leave their homes and live in the forest. The door to renunciation was sought by leaving the world. The *Sanyasins* lived by begging their way and in the ancient time, the kings used to uphold and maintain them, as a great religious order.

It is now realized that it is not necessary to leave the home for a hermitage in a secluded cave or forest to achieve renunciation. Renunciation is non-attachment of the mind to the objects of the senses and this can be achieved by living in the midst of the world. Swami Vivekananda, who was a *Sanyasi* having lived a number of years in the seclusion of a monastery, visited America and Europe in the latter part of his life and was worshipped by enthusiastic crowds of Americans as a great mystic. He lived in the world but he had no attachment to any thing, having gained complete control over this mind and body. He had gained occult knowledge but he never made use of it for any selfish purpose. His mind was fixed on God and God alone and wherever he travelled and whatever he did, he worked like a Trojan, delivering speeches, writing books, organizing *ashrams* and other religious institutions, issuing instructions for the carrying out of the purpose of the Mission, which had taken a world-wide basis, — he was playing the part of a most active mystic.

In mediaeval Europe, we know of mystics, chiefly Catholic mystics who were inclined to lead a passive life of meditation and prayers. They even believed in the mortification of the flesh. We know that Suso, the German mystic mortified his flesh for sixteen long years to get divine illumination. But the modern mysticism is different from the ancient Indian, Magian, Egyptian and Greek Mysticism. God wants us to go through the mill of life, with joyousness in our hearts, helping everyone on the way, be he of whatever faith — for all faiths lead to the same gate of God, who is the Father of us all His children. The true mystic is he, who unattached, pure in mind and body, works like a Gandhiji in the service of all mankind, his heart and mind fixed on God and God alone.

The intense longing of the soul for God is very beautifully described by the great mystic Ruysbroeck in the following passages of great significance:

"All that He has, all that He is, He gives: all that we have, all that we are, He takes."

And then again: "To eat and to be eaten: this is union." What terse language and how metaphorically does it express with a forcible precision, the hunger and thirst for God.

William Blake, a great mystic, poet and artist, speaks of this union of man with God, as mystic's marriage, after the dark night of the soul.

Nothing can run smooth in this life. But our faith and love of God should smoothen the hardest stones on the footpath of life. The dark night of the soul must give way to the dawn of the illuminating light of God.

Jalalu'Din Rumi, the great Sufi poet sings of the soul's union with God in the following very beautiful verses full of imagery:

"With Thy sweet soul, this soul of mine
Hath mixed as water doth with wine.
Who can the wine and water part
Or me and Thee, when we combine?

Thou art become my greater self;
Small bounds no more can me confine.
Thou hast my being taken on,
And shalt not I now take on Thine?

Thy love has pierced me through and through,
Its thrill with bone and nerve entwine.
I rest in flute laid on Thy lips;
A lute, I on Thy breast recline.

Breathe deep in me that I may sigh;
Yet strike my strings, and tears shall shine."

(Jalau'Din, "*The Festival of Spring.*")

Love is mutual. When we yearn for God, He also yearns for us, in fact, in a much greater measure. We get an idea of this deep, abiding love of God for all mankind, when He sent Christ on earth to reform us and to instil into us love for all that is sublime and spiritual. Deifying of man and humanizing of God with a view to create a greater fervour is the common teaching of various Catholic mystic saints. "He became man that we might be made God" said St. Athanasius. Says St. Augustine also, "I heard Thy voice from on high crying unto me, I am the Food of the full grown. Grow and then thou shalt feed on Me. Nor shalt thou change me into thy substance as thou changest the food of thy flesh, but thou shalt be changed into Me."

The mystics are the pioneers of humanity. They march along the vanguard of human progress, whether we see them as poets or pastors, artists or dreamers, soldiers or administrators. They are "giants of the spirit" who dominate all the walks of life and spread the sunshine of joy and happiness through out the length and breadth of the world. But for them the world would be a dreary place. They are our guides, our teachers, our friends, our saviours, our inspirers. They are the Ambassadors from the Court of God. A transcendent light shines off them. There is cheer in their hearts; there is joy in their eyes. They radiate love and joy and remove the pall of darkness from the earth. They live between the two worlds. They get light from the Other World and pass it on to their brothers and sisters on this plane, for the uplift of their souls. They are the witnesses of the Reality. They vindicate the triumph of the Spirit.

And yet what treatment has the world given to these pioneers of human progress and welfare. Have we not burnt Joan of Arc, — that simple peasant woman of hardly fourteen years of age who saw visions and dreams and came out boldly to save her country, France from the invasion of the English, at a critical hour. She took command of the French army and led her country's forces to victory and triumph and made the British army to retreat from St. Orleans.

We burnt Bruno, the mystical scientist for he would not recant his words nor deviate from what to him was a conviction of the soul. Was not Socratese given the cup of poison to drink, because he taught morals to the Athenian youths, bringing them nearer to God? Such is the perfidy of men !

Man is both a brute and a god. He is a brute in the initial stage of his progress. He becomes a God when the spirit finally triumphs over the flesh and finds its liberation.

The mystic's way is long and thorny, it is dark and dreary. The journey has to be made birth after birth but the pilgrim whose face is set towards Jerusalem must eventually enter into the City of God. The mystic's is not a way-ward plunge into the abyss of the Unknown. He is a pilgrim who walks with measured steps, fully aware of the fact that he is treading on the firm ground that would lead him to the City of God. The mystic's pilgrimage is the ascent of the spirit towards its own original home. It is the goal of life's journey.

God is country of the soul. The mystic develops his consciousness of the Divine within him to the highest extent. His is spiritual joy transcending all human description.

Let us cast a glance at the 'galaxy of those mystic stars, which the world has given birth to, in all ages and in all climes from the ancient to the modern times; those great Persian kings, of the most ancient age — Kaikaoos and Kaikhushru, Hoshang and Feradun, Lohrasp and Gustasp, all of whom were Yogins of the highest type; the great Hindu philosophers and yogins, — Shankaracharya and Patanjali, Swami Vivekananda and Sri Aurobindo Ghosh and innumerable others, the great Catholic saints to the medieval Europe — Suso, St.

Theresa, Eckhart, Boehme, St. Augustine, St. Francis, St. Bernard; the Greek seers, —Pythagoras and St. Orpheus; the great Sufis, — Jalal 'ud Din Rumi, Attar, Hafiz, Kabir and others; the Theosophists — Madame Blavatsky, Dr. Besant and Bishop Leadbeater. These are only a few names picked up at random from both ancient and modern history.

What do they tell us? They are the embodiments of the final triumph of the spirit over matter. They are the light bringers. They tell us by their example that the chief concern of man is not only to know God but to become one with God.

The author of *Yogavasishtha* describes the method of God-realization. Man is composed of three parts — body, mind and soul. We have therefore to look at life from three aspects, physical, mental and spiritual. The physical aspect concerns with the body, which is maintained by the movements of vital currents. The mental aspect concerns with the mental life of man, namely his thoughts, emotions and desires. The spiritual aspect corresponds according to modern thinkers to the sub-conscious self. All these three aspects, — the physical, mental and spiritual are intimately connected with one another. Now in order to rise from the finite into the infinite, we have to be above the limitations of our personality. The yoga of *Yogavasishtha* offers three methods of self-consciousness, each pertaining to the three aspects, viz. (1) Deep affirmation of the Reality, (2) mental control and (3) the control and stoppage of the activity of the *Prana*.

Of these three methods, the control of the mind is considered by Vasishtha as the best and the easiest. By deep affirmation of the Reality, what is meant is that the aspirant must meditate upon God, as the only reality and must discard everything else as *maya*. By constantly affirming to himself, "I am the Brahman," "I am the Absolute," though it may seem fantastic and vain-glorious the man's sub-conscious mind gets in tune with the Reality. He attains perfect peace.

The second method is the control of the mind. It is the mind that acts as a barrier to the realization of God. If that barrier be removed or annihilated, the road to God-realization becomes clear. The method suggested is the usual one of renunciation. As one mystic writer says, "The individual self must be lost before the Self can be found." "Love of self shuts me out from Truth and seeking their own personal happiness, they lose the deeper, purer and more abiding bliss. He, who has yielded up that self, that personality, which most men love and cling to with such fierce tenacity, has left behind him all perplexity." Individuality has to be crushed. When we cease to feel our individuality, we become conscious of universality, which is God-realization.

Renunciation of desires and pleasures of the senses, eradication of egotism, complete sense of detachment, complete renunciation of every kind of possession and constant meditation, —these are the methods for the effective control of the mind.

The third method is the control and stoppage of the activity of the *Prana*. Prana is the Sanskrit word for the vital energy of the body. According to Vashistha, the *prana* and the mind are intimately connected. What prana is in the physical plane, mind is on the psychical plane. There is complete identity between the physical and psychical side of our being. If, therefore, the movements of the prana be stopped, the mind can also be stopped from its activities. If you stop the *prana*, you stop the mind. If you stop the mind, you stop the *prana*. And in this way by controlling both the body and the mind, you reach God-realization. The stopping of the movements of the prana is a mechanical process fraught with great danger and it is not advisable for any one to resort to such a method for the attainment of the liberation of one's soul, unless the exercises are made in the presence of a *guru*, who knows all about it and can guide and check the aspirant. India is a land of mystics. The spirit of Sri Shankaracharya is still extant in this country of saffron robed *sanyasins* and yogins. Its spirituality is the hope of the new world's civilisation, — a civilisation which shall be founded upon the Gandhian method of truth and Ahimsa — a civilisation in which the aspiration of each man shall be to realize God, through *bhakti, gnan,* or *karma yoga*, the ancient fabric of Indian spirituality.

Christ taught Oneness with God. Did he not say:

"That they all may be one; as Thou
Father *art in me and I in* Thee, that
they also may be one in us: that the
world may believe that Thou hast sent me.

"And the glory which Thou gavest me,
I have given them; that they may be
one, even as we are one."

(St. John-Chapter XVII-21-22.)

The dream of the mystic is to "transcend sight and knowledge" to be wholly delivered in the bosom of the Lord. Jalalu'd Din Rumi says;

"This is love: to fly heavenward,
To rend every instant, a hundred veils,
The first moment to renounce life;
The last step, to fare without feet.
"To regard the world as invisible,

Not to see what appears to oneself."
God alone is the Reality; all else is *maya.*

GOD

Thou art the hidden spark in every man,
Whether good or bad, saint or sinner.
Thou art the hidden voice that murmurs
Like the gliding stream,
And urges man to climb the ladder, step by step,
Till he reaches the crest star.
Thou art the impelling force, the consuming ardour,

The thirst and food of the seeker,
On the endless journey.
Thou glideth from eternity to eternity;
Thou art the goal of the mystic,
His endless joy and sunshine in the dark alleys of life;

The Flute of Love, that perpetually sings
And guides the seeker to the Throne of Truth.

APPENDIX

Mystic Musings

By: M.K. Spencer

O God, Ishvara, Ahuramazda, Jehovah, Allah by whatever name be Thou called, Thou art All in All to us. Thou art Truth; Thou art Love; Thou art the Fountain of Mercy and the Throne of Justice. Thou art the Pillar of Strength; Thou art the Asylum and the Hospitable Home of every traveller, weary of body and sick in soul. Thou art the Anchor in the stormy sea of Life. Thou art the Goal of Life's Journey. Thou art the resplendent Sun, the Beacon Light, the Guiding Star to every footsore traveller. May Thou be praised for ever and ever! Amen.

Says the Rig Veda, "Dark is this path, O Bright One; bright is the light before Thee." We know the hardships of the way; we shall stumble and fall; we shall get kicks and knocks; we shall be villified and criticised. Attempts will be made to slay us, bodily and spiritually. But we shall fight and struggle against all the dark forces of *Ahreman*: we shall withstand the allurements of the senses; we shall keep fast to the commons of Thy Law. There is an inward light in the cave of every human heart. We shall keep that burning, for, it shall cheer us and help us on in the path of life. We shall hold on steadfastly to the life of austerity and purity, simplicity and beauty for, it is only in this manner that we can gain the guidance of the Elder Brothers who are so anxious to help us.

Says the Rig Veda, "What is the value of this worldly wealth to us? What is its advantage? Tell us, Jatavedas, for thou knowest what is the best course for us in this secret passage, so that we may follow the direct Path unobstructed. What is the limit, what are the objects and what is the desirable end, towards which we rush like swift chargers to the battle? When for us the divine dawns, the brides of the Immortal Sun, overspread the world with light."

(*Rig Veda* IV-V; 12 and 13).

Man's heart craves for the Absolute. The worldly pleasures are so transient that they can give no satisfaction. It is only the mystic that seeks the right path, the path of Rita, the path of Righteousness leading into Eternity. Desires and ambition, love for glory and pomp, name and fame are mere delusions. They keep us firmly rooted to this mundane world fastened to the body, to the detriment of the soul, which alone is immortal.

The path of Righteousness is as hard and narrow as the razor end. To tread this path is difficult but with the help of the Master and the sacred Scriptures, the dark and stony passage becomes luminous and smooth.

There is all joy around us, if we were but to bathe our soul in the light of God's beauty that surrounds us in nature. The sun and the moon the stars and the sky, the birds and the flowers, the zephyr that blows gently through the meadow, carrying the fragrance of the roses, the birds that chirp merrily — all speak of the universal joyousness which is the voice of God. Let us treasure this divine joyousness in our heart.

What a thrill of happiness passes through our body, when we utter the magic words prescribed in every religion to invoke God and his angels. "OM". "Tat Sat Aum", cries the Hindu Vedantist. "Ahura Mazda" is the sacred word that leaps from the heart of the Zoroastrian. The follower of Islam cries in a sonorous voice "Allahm, Allah." The Christian sings hymns in praise of God, Christ and the Virgin Mary. "The Father, Son and the Holy Ghost," forms the triple mantra.

God is not a mere concept, but an indubitable Reality — the only Real Substance, composed of Wisdom and Bliss. He is beyond human comprehension and conception.

It is only through devotion of the heart and strenuous service in aid of mankind and spiritual wisdom, combined with unselfishness of purpose, without expectation of any return or reward for one's labour that the bliss of God and the Omni-potence of God can be felt and realized. He is the Absolute Spirit. He is Infinite. How can our finite mind, comprehend that which is measureless, boundless infinite? How can we speak of His attributes, when He is indescribable, Unknowable, beyond human intellect and comprehension? It is not by reason or logic that he could be identified. But we can feel His Greatness. His Omnipotence, Omnipresence. Omniscience, by the light of Faith, Says the Bible, "We walk by Faith not by light." How beautifully the poet says:

> "I stretch lame hands of faith and grope
> And gather dust and chaff and call
> To what I feel is the Lord of All
> And faintly trust the larger hope."

As wc advance spiritually the light of the knowledge of God pours into our heart and mind, like the billows of a stormy sea, ravishing us with a joyousness of feeling beyond description.

"Infinite Ideality! Immeasurable Reality
Infinite Personality! Hallowed be Thy name!
We feel we are nothing, for all is thou and in Thee,
We feel we are something, that also has come from
Thee,
We know we are nothing, but Thou wilt help us to be,
Hallowed be Thy name!"

"I crave union with Thee, O Lord!" This is the mystic's daily cry; his daily food, his daily dress, his daily thought. He sees nothing but God; he feels nothing but God; He wants nothing but God. There is God in the bush and the tree. There is God in the bud and the child. There is god in the bird and the sky. Wherever he turns his eyes, whatever he thinks, whatever he does, it is all God. God and joyousness go ever together. They are inseparable entities.

God is the Supreme Being, the foundation and source of our life, the summit of our aspiration.

"He is thyself, yet thou art but finite and liable to error. He is eternal and sure. He is eternal truth. When once He has entered thee and become thy warrior, He will never utterly desert thee and on the day of the great peace He will become One with Thee."

(*Light on the Path,* page 51.)

God, the Eternal Spirit pervades through out the universe. He is the same both in his manifest and unmanifest form. To know God is to know the Inner World and to acquire the secret of the whole universe. Says Lord Krishna in the Gita: "O Arjuna, the wise man who knows Myself as the Supreme being knows everything and betakes himself to Me with all his being."

God, Brahman, is not a mere postulate, but He is the Real of all Reals in this world. He is so transcendental and at the same time so immanent in nature that to attribute qualities to Him and also to say that He is free from all attributes, both are correct. "There is one God hidden in all things, Omnipresent, the innerself of all beings; He is the witness of their actions, the indweller of all beings, the witness, the consciousness, the alone, free from all attributes."

(*Svetasvatara Upanishad* 6–11)

When we say, "All this is verily Brahman, for it is sprung from it, it is absorbed in it and moves in it," we attribute qualities to God; the universe is His manifestation. God is the apex and model of perfection and to attain to His divinity the best course is to meditate upon God either in His external aspect or as any of His internal qualities. The whole nature is God's garment. We may meditate upon any of His qualities, such as beauty, wisdom, mercy, love, justice. The highest mediation is when we identify ourselves completely with the Deity as our own pure self.

There is melody in the valley, there is beauty in the bower. The butterfly that hangs on the flower and the bee that gathers honey; the cuckoo that sings in the meadow and the zephy: that passes by laden with the fragrance of the rose; the sun that sends its resplendent rays on the earth below and the stars that shine at night in the azure vault of the sky, like twinkling lamps — they all speak of God's love and glory for man's happiness and bliss. Jesus says: "Raise the stone and there thou shalt find me, cleanse the wood and there am I."

"God is all." Each speck of matter has the image of the beauty and glory of God in it. How beautifully has Jami the great Persian mystic poet said:

"What heart
Doth yield to love, He charms it. In His love
The heart hath life. Longing for Him, the soul

Hath victory. That heart which seems to love
The fair ones of this world, loves Him alone.
Beware! say not, 'He is all All beautiful
And we His lovers.' Thou art but the glass
And He the face confronting it, which casts
Its image in the mirror. He alone
Is manifest, and thou in truth art hid."

The Masters are the builders of art and beauty, law and wisdom, harmony and music. To love God is to love beauty, refinement, culture, virtue, truth, purity, simplicity, naturalness, absence of egotism, childlikeness, humility, spontaneity, grace and good manners. These are the seeds of a joyous life and joyousness means divinity.

The soul always cries for God. Is it not said in the Old Testament (Psalm), "My heart crieth out for God yea, for the living God." He is really a miserable man, who has no love for God, in him. His life can not but be unlovely, coarse, frigid, stupid, silly. Says Emerson: "Unlovely, nay, almost frightful, is the solitude of the soul which is without God in the world."

With love for God, man is in unison with the highest forces in nature. Beauty and joy, peace and harmony, love and beatitude reign supreme in the human breast, when the soul shares the divine light. There is a joy of living, when the mind is engrossed in the thoughts of God. There is diffusion of light in the human soul, when it open its windows to God the only Reality, the Parent of Joy and sunshine, peace and happiness.

Without God, the soul is dark within. It is an empty terrain of lovelessness and low aims. God is the living breath. It is the nectar of life; it is the urge of the soul for the vaster realities of life. It is the cry of the soul for perfection.

Sir S. Radhakrishnan says, "We are at grips with reality in the inner depths of the soul." There is in man this persistent urge, to know God; this craving for the Eternal is natural. In each one of us, there is a certain spiritual intuition, latent most part but such that it can be actuated and made patent by contacts with evolved souls and by reading of scriptures. No logic or science can prove the existence of God. But to the mystics, God's existence is a reality. The spiritual truths given expression to by the ancient seers and Rishis are the products of their inner vision and personal experiences. The very word "Rishi" is derived from the root "*dris*" which means to see. Spiritual experiences are not chimerical vapourings of an imaginative mind but the fruits of a close communion with the Reality.

God! What a volley of ideas, this one word can raise in our mind simultaneously? What feelings of joy and delight surge in our heart?

O God ! Thou art the Divine Principle, the Supporter of the Universe, the Breath of Life, the Law of rhythm and Harmony, the "Unconditioned consciousness", the Absolute Spirit, pervading throughout the entire universe and transcending all bounds of Time, Space and Causality. Thou art One in the unmanifested form but Thou manifesteth thyself in multitudinous ways. Thou art the Fountain of Love and Mercy. Thou art the Pillar of Strength. Omnipotent, Omnipresent, Omniscient. Infinite, eternal, unchangeable, unknowable, Inexplicable, Incomprehensible, thou art One without a second, the Creator, the Unifier, the Preserver, the Destroyer, the Giver of life, the taker of life, *the summum bonum* of all human wishes. Thou art the enchanting Lord, who hears all tales of sorrow and distress, forgives sins and pours out His rays of glory on all alike whether saints or sinners. Thou bringest the erring souls to the path of righteousness.

O God, Thou art the Benevolent Master, whose hospitable Home is sought by the weary travellers on the path. Thou art Brahman to the Hindus, Buddhakaya to the Buddhists, Ahura Mazda to the Zoroastrians, Heavenly Father to the Christians, Allah to the followers of Mahamad and Jehovah to the Israels. Though professing separate faiths all of them are united in spirit, for, thou art the same Father to all of them, Thy children, without distinction of any kind. Thou art present in the garden of the heart of every devotee.

"And nothing here has power to move
My soul's tranquillity,
And life seems but a trance, a dream,
And all I feel and see
Illusion, Visionary, 'Y O U'
The One Reality."

When the *Gopis* lost their sense of personality and danced with ravishing delight with Lord krishna, they all had become Krishnas for the time being and were no longer cowherdesses. When Jesus Christ said to his disciples: "Let your light so shine before man that they may see your good works and glorify your Father which is in heaven," He did not mean the influence of good works only, but that Inner Light, "The Light of God's face." which burns in every soul, when it thinks of God and prays to God and is absorbed in God, day and night. "The Light within" is called 'The Single Eye.' It is the Sanctuary Lamp, the perpetual Light. Is it not said in the Bible: "The Spirit of man is the candle of the Lord" (Proverbs XX, 27). Serving God uninterruptedly, talking of God at every place and every where, abandoning sensuous pleasures, meditating on His nature, giving up pride and egotism, abandoning the comforts of life and practising virtues enjoined by religions, abstention from the company of the profane, the wicked and the irreligious, large-heartedness and tolerance and, above all, looking upon all as our brothers and sisters, without any sense of separateness — these are the steps to God-realization. God is all Truth; God is the purest Essence. It is by the way of truthfulness, purity of heart, unbounded love for all and unselfish service that the soul gets God-realization and it is finally merged in the Ocean of Divine Bliss. It is not by the "pride of pedigree" but the sincere devotion of heart, not by intelligence or deep learning but by wisdom born of austerity and purity can the foundation stone be laid for the mystical marriage of the soul with the spirit.

According to the *Upanishads*, rest can be obtained only when men and Gods are merged in the Absolute.

In the Christian Bible the words commonly used are: Rest, Peace, Joy, Love and Light. Christ says: "Come unto Me and I shall give you rest," "Learn of Me and ye shall find rest."

The Law of Cause and Effect works in nature and in order to earn rest, we have to work like Christ and learn from Christ's own example. What Christ meant when he said "I shall give you rest", was that He would put us in the way to acquire Rest. The effort to acquire rest is to be our own. it can not be obtained by mere desiring. It is not a treasure which is obtained "in a happy hour." We have to work for it, prepare for it, strive for it and it is only then like the morning dew, it falls upon the lap of the soul.

Christ's life, externally, was a bitter struggle against the heaviest odds of opposition. He faced persecutions, hostilities, animosities and at last he died on the scaffold, "unwept, unmourned and unhonoured" except by a few. Such was the cruel fate meted out to one who was the wisest and perfect of all men on earth. But, internally, Christ was at peace with Himself. He had inward rest. His soul was in communion with God and all the external oppositions and sufferings made no impression upon His spirit. He was calm and serene like the silent waters of the deep sea. Peace and rest cannot be obtained unless we prepare ourselves for all emergencies and strive like Christ to do our best for the good of others. Inward calm and inward peace are the results of hard knocks, patiently borne with resignation to the will of God. If we can say with Browning, "God's in His Heaven, all's well with the world," there is no tempest or opposition that can disquieten or disturb the tranquillity of our mind and soul.

Rest should not be mistaken for stagnation. Two artists painted two different pictures to give an idea of rest and peace. One painter, painted the picture of a lake in the solitude of encircling mountains, serene and calm. The other artist painted a waterfall, thundering down with a huge velocity from the top of the mountain and at the end of the edge of the foam, there is a delicate birch tree and on one of its branches a robin is seen sitting near the swirling water quite unconcerned and fearless of the tempest blowing. Internal tranquillity comes from fearlessness and it was one of the chief characteristics of Christ, whose life is a lesson to us in all respects.

Christ came not to give any new teaching but to awaken us from deep slumber, to inflame our minds to live a full life, a true life, an abundant life, "a life that is life indeed." It is said, the influence of Christ was so great that those who came in contact with Him were completely transformed. Even the fishermen who followed Him changed their lives and became sinless. Purity of heart and love formed the basic teaching of Christ. Christ was all Love and Purity, just as God is Love and Essence of Purity.

There is a very significant passage in the Bible on which we shall ruminate:

"Though I speak with the tongues of men and of angels, and have not Love, i am become as sounding brass, or a tinkling cymbal.

And though I have the gift of prophecy, and understand all mysteries, and all knowledge and though I have all faith, so that I could remove mountains and have not Love, I am nothing.

And though I bestow all my goods to feed the poor and though I give my body to be burned and have not Love, it profiteth me nothing.

Love suffereth long and is kind; Love envieth not; Love vaunteth not itself, is not puffed up.

Doth not behave itself unseemly, seeketh not her own, is not easily provoked, thinketh no evil;

Rejoiceth not in iniquity, but rejoiceth in the truth;

Beareth all things, believeth all things, hopeth all things endureth all things.

Love never faileth; but whether there be prophecies, they shall fail; whether there be tongues, they shall cease; whether there be knowledge, it shall vanish away.

For we know in part and we prophesy in part.

But when that which is perfect is come, then that which is in part shall be done away.

When I was a child, I spoke as a child; I understood as a child; I thought as a child; but when I became a man, I put away childish things.

For now we see through a glass, darkly; but then face to face; now I know in part; but then I shall know even as also I am known.

And now abideth faith, hope, love, these three; but the greatest of these is Love"

(*1 Corinthians, Chapter* 13.)

In the original text the word used is "charity" but we have used the word "Love" which is more significant and which really speaking is meant by Christ. The above passage is the finest expression of thought that we find in the whole Bible. In fact, Christ Himself is the highest embodiment of Love, which he made the principal teaching of His religion. It is a matter for argument whether Love should be considered as the greatest thing in religion or Faith. In no religion of the world is so great importance paid to Love as in Christianity. With what rapture Christ says, "God is Love" and "Love is the fulfilling of the Law". All the ten commandments are included in that one word "Love." If we love every one, we can not but be unselfish, pure, righteous, kind and gentle, free from jealousy, generous to the fault, humble and even tempered, wise and discerning. The whole character of Christ is based and built round Love. "To love abundantly is to live abundantly and to love for ever is to live for ever. Hence eternal life is inextricably bound up with love" (Henry Drummond's "*The Greatest thing in the Word*" page 49).

Love is grater than eloquence, greater than prophecy, greater than faith, greater than charity, greater than hope. Henry Drummond in his remarkable survey includes in love the following qualities:

Patience: "Love suffering long"
Kindness: "And is kind."
Generosity: "Love enricheth not."
Humility: "Love vaunteth not itself, is not puffed up."
Courtesy: "Doth not behave itself unseemly."
Unselfishness: "Seeketh not her own."
Good Temper: "Is not easily provoked."
Guilelessness: "Thinketh no evil."
Sincerity: "Rejoiceth not in iniquity but rejoiceth in the truth."

Love is patient; love is active; love is unselfish. It never fails. It is the energy of life. It is the destroyer of jealousy, anger, pride, uncharity, cruelty, self-righteousness, touchiness, doggedness, smallness.

Love is spiritual energy; love is life. It is supreme in nature, because it is an Eternal Life. "He that dwelleth in love dwelleth in God. For God is love." He who loves is born of God.

What is the test of religion? Not religiousness but love which is an all embracing and all transforming factor in life. To love is to be Christ-like. To with-hold love is to deny the spirit of Christ. It is negation of Christ. Not to save one's own soul only but also to save the souls of others, to make the world a happier and better place to live in, for all is the real concern of religion.

To spread the joyousness of life is the design of God and it was mainly Christ's mission to plant in the hearts of men the seeds of love and kindliness, gentility and sincerity, piety and humility, for the liberation of the whole world from the prison of the flesh. He taught man the true art of life.

Let us meditate upon the following aphorisms culled from the Vedas:

1. "You" is hell, "I" is hell.
   Put off, wear holy shell.
2. Cease fuss of "You" and "I"
   And thought of low and high.
3. One Essence permeates all
   Is delusion big or small.
4. Unreal are name and form
   Things does time deform.
5. Nothing stays, view evanascent
   Alike sentient and insentient.

6. God alone is permanent
   Unstill the rest's temperament.
7. "That thou art" Vedanta says,
   To which homage logic pays.
8. Realize this wishing freedom
   To render asunder Maya's thraldom.
9. When Maya's bondage one breaks,
   "I am God" he cheerfully states.
10. Thereafter he lives in perfect peace
   Mindless of cold and heat."

A PRAYER

O God, Thou art the Sustainer and Supporter of the universe. The sun and the stars, the blue vault of the sky and the planes that revolve in the Solar System are Thy manifest creations.

Thou hast created Law and Order;
Thou hast made the spheres sing the songs of the celestial
Men and Angels worship Thee in deep reverence and love,
For they know, that by the path of devotion and service can Thou be realized.
Thy power is eternal, Thy name is Holy
Thou hast tabernacles in the hearts of men,
Who worship Thee, ever and anon.
Men's greatness of achievements pales into insignificance before Thy might and main.
All things perish; Thou alone art Real and unperishable.
We shall out assunder the veil that hides the secrets of the universe.

We shall sing Thy praises; we shall work unostentatiously.
For it is by the way of *Nishkama*, that we shall realize Thee.
Four Thou Thy rays of beneficence and wisdom upon us
Thy children who long for Thee, O Lord.
May we be bathed in the Glory of Thy Light!
We shall renounce everything for by renunciation
And in utter nakedness, shall we find Thee, O Lord.
O God, may we arise from the tabernacle of the flesh.
O God, may we hear the sweet voice of the music of the stars.
O God, may we not slumber in the sickening shadows of pride and prejudice.
O God, brighten our souls with the joy of Thy Love.
O God, quicken the heart and mind and fill us with the rhapsody of the song of self forgetfulness.
The sunshine of life comes in, when Thy grace abideth in us.

A Brief Profile of Minocher K. Spencer

M.K. Spencer (1888–1958) was a great Yogi, perfect medium and above-all a great Spiritualist. He was born in the Parsee community in India. He was the resident of Karachi, now in Pakistan. He was a metal merchant by profession. This was his third and last birth as a human being in this world. He had the guidance of Rishi Ram — A Great Master of the Spirit World, even while he was in his cradle. On reaching higher stage in his spiritual evolution, the change of his spiritual training was taken over by Sri Shirdi Sai Baba till the last stage of his God realization.

His goal was to see God face to face, and to be with Him side by side. In the last stage, he was spending eighteen hours in meditation daily, and the balance of six hours he spent in taking food, rest, writing on spiritual topics and serving lepers and this was his hobby. As ordained by God, he had written more than 2000 pages of typed matter on the topic "*How I Found God.*" and Foreword given by God. One hundred copies of the same were printed by the Spiritual Healing Centre, Coimbatore in 1953, but before that interesting, illuminating and thrilling book could be released for the benefit of the devotees, it was God's order to burn all the said books, written in the course of one month. This incident was a shocking experience and it was like asking a mother to kill her newborn child. This was another given to him to test whether there was any grain of egoism and he withstood this test successfully.

The Spiritual Healing Centre, Coimbatore (closed down in January 1965) had published the following valuable books of M.K. Spencer:

1. *Religion in Life*, 270 pages.
2. *Hymns*, 166 pages
3. *Life's Philosophy*, 160 pages.
4. *Oneness With God.*, 350 pages.
5. *Light on The Path*, 250 pages.
6. *Joyous Mysticism*, 450 pages.
7. *The Other World*, 260 pages.
8. *Divine Discourses and Poems*, 156 pages.

In his autobiographical book '*Romance of a Soul*' (1954) published by the Spiritual Healing Centre, Coimbatore, M.K. Spencer revealed the following thrilling details about his three births objectively in third person as gathered by him from God.

First Birth in 1213 as Petrioio

In the year of grace 1213, there was born in the house of a baron, a feudal lord. A child, whom its parents christened by the name of Petricio.

The child grew up into a very shy and reserved boy. He was quite unlike other children, especially his brothers, who loved sport and manly games of shooting and hunting. Petricio loved silence and solitude from the very commencement of his life . . . . He often felt thrilled when a sort of ecstatic joy swept him in his hours of silence and seclusion.

The boy grew up with a yearning for the Invisible. He made nature the object of deep contemplation . . . . His father wanted him to enter into some profession, but the boy as he grew in years, did not show the least inclination to any line of avocation. The parents were much disappointed. One day, he left the parental roof, leaving a note behind that he had made the world as his home and God, his protector. He wandered from place to place . . . . Wherever he went, he sang the songs composed by him and played on the flute he carried. He spoke to the people who gathered round him of God and God alone . . . . He began to collect friends. They followed him also from place to place. They formed a band of pilgrims, who made the object of their lives to talk of God and God alone and create a sort of religious awakening.

As years passed by, Petricio's fame as an itinerant preacher spread far and wide throughout Italy and even in other countries of Europe. He soon founded an Order of Friars and built a monastery. This building in spite ravages of time still exists, though in a dilapidated condition.

. . . Holy and religious as he was, he fell a victim to the notion that the church founded by him was the only way to reach God. He led a fierce and fiery crusade against all those who differed from his religious views . . . . When this good and holy man passed away in the year 1339, a spell of silence fell on the whole countryside. He was deeply loved and revered by millions of people. He was canonised thirty years after his death as a great saint of Christianity.

. . . His whole life from the cradle to grave may be considered as a romance. And yet this man, though canonised as a saint, had to take birth again. He was holy in the eyes of the world but it was holiness not of the transparent hue. It was holiness stained by the sin of religious bigotry.

. . . The prelate when he died, did come over to the Spirit World with joyous delight . . . he was ushered straight of into the highest region of the Spirit World, admissible to human souls. Here he spent a long time . . . . His soul was fully trained and equipped with powers with a view to attaining success in its next incarnation on the earth plane.

Second Birth as A Hindu Woman in Southern India

. . . God gave him a chance to earn his emancipation by giving him a birth in a totally different environment and in a different fait.

The child was a female child . . . . The child grew up into a maiden and blossomed into a sweet womanhood. The beauty of her soul was rare. She married but her married life was a dismal affair. She married, though totally averse to marriage, for the simple reason that the custom of her society left her no choice. She was, in fact, sold in marriage by her parents. Hardly when she was out of her teens, she was given away as a bride to a person more than double her age and for whom she had no liking, no reverence, no respect, no fondness. Her father's world was law and she had to bound down to his will. There was no joy in her heart when she married. She thought she was joined with a log of wood. It was not her marriage ceremony but ascending the funeral pyre. But her sense of duty was so great, that after she was forced in marriage to the man, she did not like, she greeted him as her lord and obeyed him and served him faithfully. She bore children and countered difficulties and torments, few would undergo with such heroism of spirit and sacrifice as she did. Unlettered and illtaught, she knew more of God and His divinity than all the learned *pundits* of her time. Her power of intuition was great and that was her guiding principle. Her heart was open to every cry of pain and anguish. She succoured to the poor and was always by the beside of the ailing. Her life was a continuous round of service for which she got no applause except mute gratitude of the hundreds and thousands whom she relieved of their pain and suffering.

. . . She led a life of long drawn-out agony but brave and noble as she was, she never uttered a word of complaint to any one . . . . her heart over-flowed with the milk of human kindness . . . . She considered all forsaken children as her own. She mothered them and brought solace and check to countless homes. She was looked upon as *Avatar* of God in the slums she visited, by the denizens of the dark dens. She was a veritable goddess, so thoughtless and regardless of her own gain and so imbued with the pain and suffering of others.

This woman would have gained her emancipation but being a mother, her motherly instincts, she could not conquer. She was extremely indulgent to her children and spoiled them. Her extreme love and affection for them made her overlook their faults. They were antithesis to her character. They were a constant source of anxiety to her. . . . Her up-bringing of them was wrong. . . .

God wants man to act in an unattached manner. Attachment is a sin. The woman's attachment to her children was the cause of her failure to secure emancipation of her soul, which she in all other respects she had already gained . . . . When the woman passed away there was no obituary in any paper.

Third Birth in 1988 as M.K. Spencer

On the 4th October 1888, in the city of Poona in India, the same soul which in its past incarnations had gathered experiences as a Cathohic priest and a Hindu woman, took birth in a Parsi family, following Zoroastrian faith ....

Born in a Paris home, the boy grew up in the traditions of the home and his race. Shy and backward, he still had no idea of conception of the future .... Had he wished, he could have amassed wealth, married a society woman, reared children and gained name and fame. He was however was saved from the world's *maya*, because of his experience in the past incarnations. The majority suffer because of their past *karma*. He had very little of *karma* to wipe off and when this was done. He was taken charge of a Master immediately, under God's orders.

The last five or six years of this soul (from 1948 to 1954) of this man's life make a most romantic history. It is a real, thrilling romance of the soul. He was gripped with a secret longing for God. All the latent virtues which he had inherited from his past births blossomed out into full growth. He left business. He cut himself away from all the giddy ways of the world. He took to a life of solitude, prayer and meditation, making home, God's altar, his heart, God's temple.

.... His love to probe into the mysteries of the universe increased with every step he took. . . it brought him into contact with Westers and Spirits in the higher Regions. God ordered Spirit Master Rishi Ram Ram to take under his special protection.

A new method was devised whereby he could contact and hear spirits without physical frustration and mental disorder. . . .

It was Ram Ram who made him pay visits to two God-realised souls on the earth place, *viz.*, Meher Baba and Sri Ramana. The former only ignited his soul to make an assault of the invisible World with greater furty and force. But the latter quickened his soul for *nirvana*, which he gained after his visit to the seer's *ashram* in Arunachala . . . . He gave up everything entirely. He gave up even his leper work in which he was totally absorbed. it was all planned by God. He took to solitude and deep contemplation and meditation. Continuous contact with his Master Ram Ram and the study of the Scriptures, which enabled him to write a series of books on Spiritual Philosophy and Religion. Ram Ram developed his soul to such an extent that Ram Ram was ordered by Ahura Mazda (in the form of Fakir Sai Baba) to relax his training and hand over the aspirant for further training to God Himself.

. . . Such is the simple story of this soul which is speeding fast towards the fulfilment of God's order to be His messenger on the earth before it is called away to the Other World — the home eternal. . . . Ram Ram, Christ, Zoroaster, Buddha and Lord Krishna are the guiding angels whom God has appointed to help this youthful soul in this performance of God's mission. These Masters are his guides and friends. It is to stop another world war breaking out, to establish peace on earth and to introduce religio-socio-politico and economic revolutionary changes which are so greatly needed that God is sending this emissary of Love and Goodwill for the welfare and uplift of the people of the world, torn and worn out, depressed and depraved by the vicious circle in which the world is moving so relentlessly and callously."

— Extracts from '*Romance of a Foul*' (1956)

BIBLIOGRAPHY

Eliphas Levi, *The Paradoxes of the Highest Science.*
Arthur Edward Waile, *The Occult Sciences.*
Dr. Mrs. Annie Besant, *Mysticism.*
Dr. Mrs. Annie Besant, *Avataras.*
Dr. Mrs. Annie Besant, *The Masters.*
Dr. Mrs. Annie Besant, *H.P. Blavatsky & the Masters of the Wisdom.*
Dr. Mrs. Annie Besant & C.W. Leadbeater, *Talks on the Path of Occultism.*
Madame Blavatsky, *The Secret Doctrine.*
Madame Blavatsky, *Isis Unveiled.*
Madame Blavatsky, *The Voice of the Silence.*
C. W. Leadbeater, *The Masters & the Path.*
C. W. Leadbeater, *The Hidden Side of Things.*
Cyrill Scott, *An Outline of Modern Occultism.*
Cyrill Scott, *The Initiate.*
Cyrill Scott, *The Initiate in the Dark Cycle.*
Cyrill Scott, *The Adept of Galilee.*
A Pupil (Cyrill Scott), *The Initiate in the New World.*
Edward Schure, *The Great Intitiates* (Two Vols.).
A Pupil, *Light on the Path.*

A Pupil, *Vision of the Nazarene*.
William James, *The Varieties of Religious Experience*.
Geoffrey Hadson, *Meditations on the Occult Life*.
Geoffrey Hadson, *Thus Have I heard*.
A.P. Sinnet, *The Growth of the Soul*.
A.P. Sinnet, *Occult Essays*.
A.P. Sinnet, *Esoteric Buddhism*.
Alexander Davis Neel, *With Mystics and Magicians in Tibet*.
Alexander Davis Neel, *Initiations & Initiates*.
A. J. Appasamy and B. H. Strecter, *The Sadhu* (A study in Mysticism & Practical religion).
Johan Wien, *Bible Mysteries*.
Edouard Schure, *Hermes & Plato*.
Cyrill Scott, *The Great Awareness*.
L.W. Rogers, *Hints to Young Students of Occultism*.
Daisy E. Grove, *The Mystery Teaching of the Bible*.
Kavel Weinfurter, *Man's Highest Purpose*.
Burnett Hillman Streeter, *Reality*.
Clifford Harrison, *Notes on the Margin*.
W. Marsham Adams, *The House of the Hidden Places*.
Karl Von, Eckartshansen *The Cloud upon the Sanctuary*.
Daisy E. Grove, *The Apocalypse & Initiation*.
Dr. Franz Hartman, *Magic White & Black*.
Rudolf Steiner, *Mysteries of the Renaisance*.
Shuddhanand Bharati, *Alwar Saints*.
Sri Ramanasram Golden Jubilee Souvenir.
Evelyn Underhill, *Concerning the Inner Life*.
Everlyn Underhill, *Mysticism* (A study in the Nature and Development of Man's Spiritual consciousness).
Lewis Spence, *The Mysteries of Egypt*.
Nusserwanji F. Billimoria, *Zoroastrianism in the Light of Theosophy*.

Jethmal Parasram Gulraj, *Sind & Its Sufis.*

Prof Martin Baber, *Jewish Mysticism* (translated from the German by Lewis Cohen).

J. Ralston Skinne, *Key to Hebrew— Egyptian Mystery.*

Isabel Cooper Cakley, *Mystical Traditions.*

Sa'd-ud-din Mahmud Shabistari, *Gulshan I Raz* (Mystic Rose Garden) (translated by E.H. Whimfield).

Kalyana —Kalpataru, *God Number, 1934.*

C. Jinarjadasa, *The Nature of Mysticism.*

Robert (rosbie), *Friendly Philosopher.*

Sadhu Sundersingh, *The Spiritual Life & the Spiritual World.*

Henry Drummond, *The Greatest Thing in the World.*

K. T. Telang, *Shankaracharya, Philosopher & Mystic Three Great Acharyas* (Sankara, Ramanuja & Madhwa).

Aldous Huxley, *The Perennial Philosophy.*

Julia Seton, *The Mystic's Goal.*

Works of Swami Vivekananda. Publications of the Spiritual Healing Centre, Coimbatore.

J. Krishnamurti, *At the Feet of the Master.*

Henry Metcalf, *The Evolution of Spiritualism.*

Wisdom of Silver birch being messages from the Spirit Land (Two Vols.).

Advaita Ashrama, *A Short Life of Sri Ramakrishna.*

C. Jinrajadasa,. *The Divine Vision.*

C. Jinrajadasa, *The New Humanity of Intuition* .

Diwan Bahadur K.S. and Ramaswami Sastri, *The Evolution of Indian Mysticism.*

Jethmal Parsram Gulraj, *Sind & its Sufis*
Prof. Martin Buber, *Jewish Mysticism* (translated from the German by Lewis Cohen)
Ralston Skinner, *Key to Hebrew – Egyptian Mystery*
Isabel Cooper Oakley, *Mystical Traditions*
Sa'd-ud-din Mahmud Shabistari, *Gulshan-i-Raz* (Mystic Rose Garden) (translated by E.H. Whinfield)
Kalyana—Kalpataru, *God Number 1934*
C. Jinarajadasa, *The Nature of Mysticism*
Robert Crosbie, *Friendly Philosopher*
Sadhu Sundersingh, *The Spiritual Life & the Spiritual World*
Henry Drummond, *The Greatest Thing in the World*
K. T. Telang, *Shankaracharya, Philosopher & Mystic Three Great Acharyas* (Sankara, Ramanuja & Madhva)
Aldous Huxley, *The Perennial Philosophy*
Julia Seton, *The Mystic's God*
Works of Swami Vivekananda, Publications of the Spiritual Healing Centre, Coimbatore
J. Krishnamurti, *At the Feet of the Master*
Henry Metcalf, *The Evolution of Spiritualism*
Wisdom of Silver Birch being messages from the Spirit Land (Two Vols.)
Advaita Ashrama, *A Short Life of Sri Ramakrishna*
C. Jinarajadasa, *The Divine Vision*
C. Jinarajadasa, *The New Humanity of Intuition*
Diwan Bahadur K.S. and Ramaswami Sastri, *The Evolution of Indian Mysticism*